BASIC SAILING

BASIC SAILING

BY M. B. GEORGE

Photos by Peter Barlow
Illustrations by Hank Iken

Hearst Marine Books / New York / 1984

ACKNOWLEDGMENTS

My thanks and deepest appreciation are extended to the staff of Hearst Marine Books for the research, advice, technical suggestions, and editorial accuracy that was contributed to this new edition. Special recognition goes to Queene Hooper, who was instrumental in developing this project.

—M. B. GEORGE

Contents

Introduction

Sailing is an old and complex art, and sailors can spend a lifetime at it and still find there is more to learn. It is also a simple and fairly safe activity. As a beginning sailor you can have a fine time in a sailboat on your first day out, provided you take a few precautions regarding the weather and your safety on the water. *Basic Sailing* has for years been the best source of written instruction for beginning sailors everywhere, and with this revision it remains the most up-to-date and the simplest text available for those first days under sail.

Since 1959, when the first edition of *Basic Sailing* was published, nearly half a million copies of this book have been purchased by those who want to become sailors. Now, with the book in its twenty-fifth year of publication, the editors at Hearst Marine Books have undertaken a major revision of both the text and the illustrations to bring them up-to-date.

With the advent of modern lightweight materials and simpler, faster sailboats, beginning sailors today need different instruction from those a generation ago. This revision of *Basic Sailing* continues to provide exactly what they need to start sailing. The simple straightforward approach that has made the book the choice of sailing schools, Power Squadron classes, and United States Coast Guard Auxiliary classes for twenty-five years continues to make *Basic Sailing* the first choice for everyone in need of a primer on small boat sailing.

Here you will find the basic information needed to get under way; raise the sails; trim the sails; tack, jibe, furl, reef, and douse the sails; plus how to moor, how to anchor, how to coil line, how to tie the basic knots, and what to do if you capsize.

More advanced information may be found in the complete boating reference book *Piloting, Seamanship, and Small Boat Handling,* by Charles F. Chapman, also published by Hearst Marine Books.

1

The Boat

Sailboats vary greatly in size, rig, and complexity, but the kind most beginners first learn to sail is a boat about 14 to 18 feet long with an open cockpit, a single mast, two sails, a centerboard, and a rudder controlled by a tiller.

The Hull

The *hull* is the main body of the boat—the part that floats on the water. It's generally made of fiberglass these days, although some sailboats are of wood or aluminum. The *bow* of the boat is the front, or the pointy end, and the *stern* is the back end. When you're in the boat facing the bow, the *starboard* side is on your right, and the *port* side is on your left. The hull may be entirely open, with no areas enclosed, but the most common arrangement is a small deck that covers the area ahead of the mast (called the foredeck) and side decks. In small boats the crew generally sits in the bottom of the boat within the cockpit or up on the side decks.

Rigging

A tall wooden or aluminum *mast* holds up the sails. It may be freestanding like a flagpole, or it may be supported by *standing rigging*—wires that keep it from going over the side. Standing rigging consists of *shrouds* on each side, the *forestay* (from the top of the mast to the boat's bow), and the *backstay* (from the top of the mast to the stern).

Figure 1. **This cruising boat looks and is very complicated, but she operates on the same principles as the simple boat on the facing page.**

Figure 2. Here are the basic terms for the parts on a sailboat.

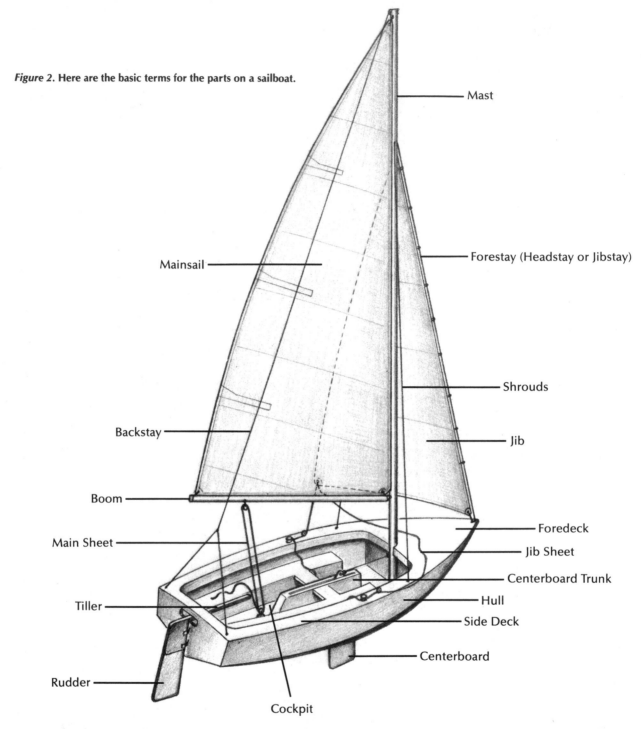

Mast

Forestay (Headstay or Jibstay)

Mainsail

Shrouds

Jib

Backstay

Boom

Foredeck

Main Sheet

Jib Sheet

Centerboard Trunk

Hull

Tiller

Side Deck

Centerboard

Rudder

Cockpit

Running rigging is lines (ropes) that raise and lower the sails and control their angle to the wind. They are adjusted frequently under sail, and it is important to know their names. The lines that raise sails are called *halyards;* those that control the sail are called *sheets.* These are found on all sailboats; there are other more complex pieces of running rigging that will be discussed later.

Most boats have a *boom,* a low horizontal spar that holds out the foot of the sail. Always be aware of the boom's position, especially when maneuvering; it can give a nasty knock on the head to anyone who forgets to duck when it swings across the boat. It is attached to the mast by a hingelike fitting called a *gooseneck,* and it is controlled by the *mainsheet.*

Centerboard or Keel

In the hull, a pivoted *centerboard* or sliding removable *daggerboard* will extend down through the middle. This board keeps the boat from sliding sideways through the water, and it is an important element in the forces that help a boat sail, as will be described in Chapter 2. For a beginner it is important to remember that the board should be in its *down* position most of the time.

If your boat doesn't have a board, she will have a fixed *keel*, which you can't see from the deck, but which extends quite far below the hull. If you haven't seen the keel on the boat you're on, ask someone how deep it goes in the water, because you must always have at least that much water under the boat so you won't run aground. This is called the boat's *draft*, or how much the boat *draws*. A keel also contains extra weight, usually lead, in its lowest section, to increase stability.

Usually larger boats, say over 20 feet, will have a keel and *ballast* instead of a centerboard, for the important advantage of stability due to the counterbalancing effect of the weight.

Figure 3. The centerboard boat obtains lateral resistance with the movable centerboard, seen above and in the upper drawing to the left. The keel on the boat in the lower photo has stability in the form of ballast in the lowest part of the keel.

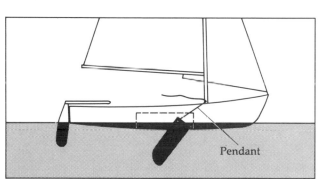

Pendant

Centerboard Hull

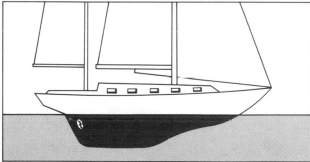

Keel Hull

Figure 4. This skipper should be thinking about how much water the boat draws before he runs aground in shallow water.

Figure 5. A deep keel on this large oceangoing vessel gives her stability in any conditions.

A centerboard (or daggerboard) *trunk* is the watertight housing in the hull in which the board is raised and lowered. It must be of strong construction and well sealed or it will be a source of leaks.

Steering

A *rudder* controlled by a lever called a *tiller* is used to steer the boat. On large sailboats the tiller may be replaced by a *wheel* which is geared to the rudder and operates just like a car's steering wheel. The tiller or wheel and therefore the rudder must be free to move at all times. Don't let the crew or stray lines entangle or obstruct its movement.

Note that the boat does not follow her bow around in the way a car follows the front wheels. The boat's bow turns in the direction you want it to go, and the stern swings the other way. There is a sliding or skidding effect. This sliding effect is important to remember when you are sailing close to another boat, rounding a buoy, or turning into a marina. Remember that the stern swings wider in a turn.

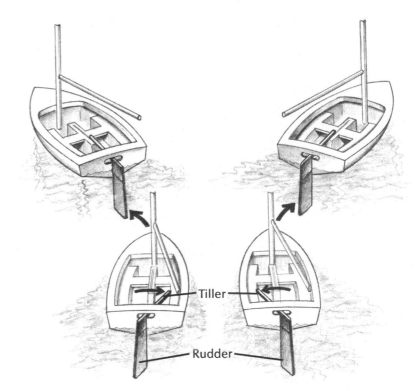

Figure 6. At first it may seem strange to push the tiller opposite to the direction you wish the boat to go, but it all makes sense soon enough.

Figure 7. The wheel instead of a tiller on large boats allows fingertip control for the helmsman. The rudder is visible under the stern.

Figure 8. With one hand on the tiller, the helmsman checks the sails and constantly watches the waters ahead.

Sails

The basic sails used on a boat are the large *mainsail* set behind the mast and the *jib* that is set ahead of the mast. The mainsail is usually triangular in shape (Figure 9), though there are other types of mainsails, described later in Chapter 6. There are many sails that may be set ahead of the mast, such as *genoas* and *spinnakers,* also described later. The jib is the basic *headsail,* and you should become familiar with its use and handling before going on to the more complex sails.

Sails are what convert the wind's energy into speed and make a boat move forward. Knowledge of their parts, how and of what they are made, and their proper use is therefore important.

A sail is composed of panels of dacron material sewn together to a prescribed size and shape. Until the advent of dacron in the 1950's, sails were made of cotton, which stretched unevenly if too much pressure was applied. Sails now are extremely durable; but they can tear easily if exposed to sharp edges, excessive chafe, or hot cigarettes; and they deteriorate rapidly if left in direct sunlight for long periods of time, say a few months.

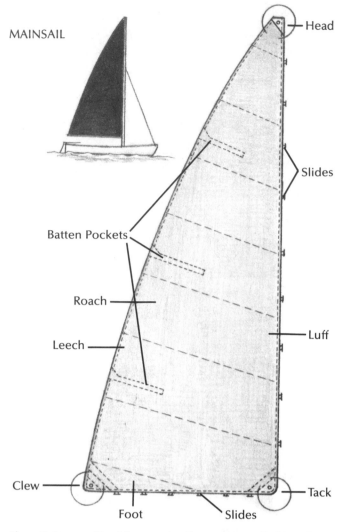

MAINSAIL

Head
Slides
Batten Pockets
Roach
Leech
Luff
Clew
Foot
Slides
Tack

Figure 9. Every sailboat has a mainsail, sometimes called just the main. These are the terms used to describe the edges and corners on the sail.

Figure 10. This jib has a spar at its foot, called a club, for ease of handling.

Mainsail

Figure 9 shows a typical mainsail. Note that each edge and each corner has its own name. Some are quite reasonable, such as *head* and *foot*, and others you need to memorize in order to learn to set and handle the sail. Note also that no edge of the sail is straight—a curve has been cut into each side to give a proper shape to the sail when it is set. Most noticeable will be the curve on the *leech*, called the *roach*, which is such a pronounced curve that it requires special *battens* to hold it out, described below. Further details of a mainsail, such as reef points, boltrope, and slides, will be discussed in Chapter 3.

Jibs

Not all boats carry a *jib*, and if your boat wasn't designed for one, you can skip this section. Most boats carry a jib, if not several types of jibs for

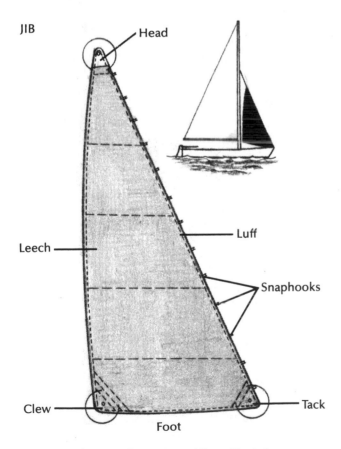

JIB

Figure 11. These are the terms used for a jib. If the corners are labeled correctly on the sail, there is less risk of setting the sail upside down.

different conditions, because it adds sail area and sailing ability to a boat. In some boats the jib will be as large or even larger than the mainsail and overlap it. It is then called a *genoa jib*.

The standard jib is often called the *working jib*. It is the ordinary sail that fits in the *foretriangle*, the triangle formed by the mast, the foredeck, and the *jibstay* (head stay).

Terms for a jib are shown in Figure 11. Most jibs have no boom to extend the foot of the sail, although some cruising boats may carry a boom or *club* to simplify sail handling. The jib is attached directly onto the jibstay, or forestay as it is often called, by means of special spring-loaded hooks called either *snap hooks* or *hanks*. Large racing boats may employ a special groove on the forestay for fast sail changes, but most small boats rely on hanks. The tack is secured to a hook at the base of the forestay, and the head to the jib halyard shackle.

The jib will have two sheets, one on each side of the mast. Only one is ever used at one time; the other will be slack. Each will lead from the corner of the jib outboard; around the shrouds (some boats have jib sheets that lead inside the shrouds, depending on chafe points and the size of the jib); and to a lead block (or on small boats, a fairlead—an eye fitting on the deck) on an adjustable track. Proper sheet lead is important for a good sail shape—more on determining that lead will be described later. After the lead block, the sheet may go directly to the cockpit, to a winch, or to a cleat there, to be controlled and constantly trimmed by the crew.

Battens

Battens are used in a mainsail to stiffen the rounded roach of the sail. Battens are tied in place in their pockets or inserted at an angle to their pockets through an opening in the leech. The thicker end goes at the edge of the sail.

Battens are often of different lengths and should be numbered or lettered to correspond to their respective pockets. The longer battens are usually the two middle ones.

Because of their thinness and the risk of ripping the sail material, battens should be removed from a

Figure 12. Battens help to hold out the rounded roach of the sail. This boat has battens on the jib as well as on the mainsail.

sail when it is bagged if possible. If you leave battens in the sail, be sure to fold or roll the sail without damaging the battens. Keep them parallel to each other to prevent damage.

The Tiller and Rudder

The modern small sailboat is easy to steer. The tiller should be held at its extreme end, not in the middle. In a well-balanced craft the tiller can be controlled by the fingertips, but as the wind increases, a firm grip may be needed on the tiller. It should never be jerked back and forth. Steering movements should be smooth; the less movement the better because an angled rudder slows the boat.

The tiller is always moved in a direction *opposite* where you want the bow to move. If the boat is to go to port, the tiller is moved to starboard; if she is to go to starboard, the tiller is moved to port.

A *tiller extension*, or *hiking stick*, a short bar at the end of the tiller, is used when the skipper has to be out on the rail in strong winds. When not needed, it lies snugly on top of the tiller and looks like part of the tiller.

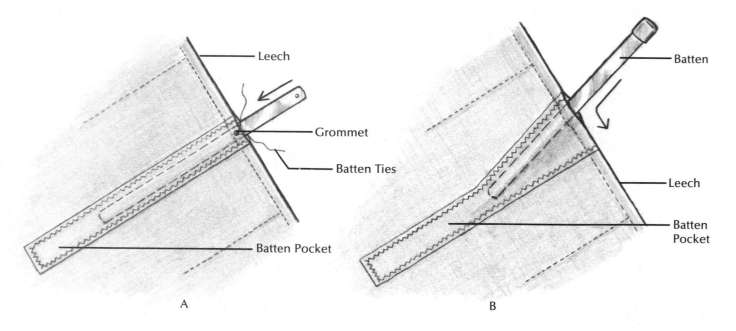

Figure 13. Battens are held in their pockets in the sail by short ties, or by an angled opening.

Figure 14. Hiking out and using the tiller extension, these sailors are bringing their boat into the harbor on her feet and at top speed.

Helpful Hints

THE CENTERBOARD

- It moves forward when lowered and moves aft when raised. It pivots on a pin through its forward lower corner. Position is changed by hauling or easing a pendant attached to the upper corner.

- Centerboards generally are rectangular in shape, longer than they are wide, but sometimes on large boats they take the shape of a pie wedge.

- The centerboard trunk extends into the cockpit, dividing it into two parts. The trunk needs strong construction as the crew's feet are braced against it.

- It requires a larger opening in the keel than does a daggerboard, thereby creating greater underwater friction.

- Should an underwater object be hit, the board normally will swing up out of harm's way.

- It is always housed or partly housed in its trunk except when all the way down.

- As it is adjusted, there is greater spread in its fore-and-aft movement and in the center of lateral resistance, thus necessitating sail trimming and changes in crew's position.

THE DAGGERBOARD

- It moves straight up and down, not on a pivot, by hand alone. It can be awkward to handle, particularly when the boat is heeled and strong side pressure is exerted.

- It is long and narrow in shape and lighter in weight than a centerboard as a rule. Sometimes some of the board is cut away.

- The daggerboard trunk is placed well forward, thereby allowing more room for movement in the cockpit. It is easier to brace when it is structurally tied in with the foredeck.

- It allows for a smaller opening in the keel, thereby reducing the underwater friction compared to that of a centerboard.

- If the daggerboard hits an underwater object, the boat may come to a jarring halt, and the board may be severely damaged.
  When lowered, it is exposed below water as much as a centerboard, but when raised, it extends upward to just below the boom and gets in the way of the sheets and boom vang.

- The center of lateral resistance moves in a narrower range, because the board goes only one way—straight down.

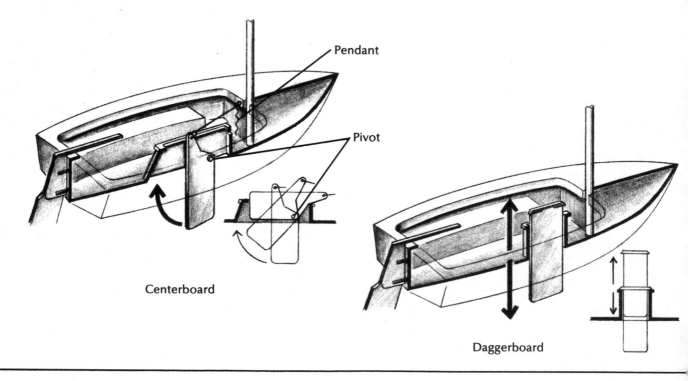

Pendant

Pivot

Centerboard

Daggerboard

Figure 15. Leeboards are effective in preventing sideslip and are simple to construct. They have been used on boats of all sizes for many years.

LEEBOARDS

Sailing canoes and some dinghies use leeboards, a system similar in principle to a centerboard. Leeboards reduce leeway just as well as a centerboard. As shown above, a board is placed on each side of the boat; and the two boards are bolted to an athwartship bar. The bolts are tightened enough to hold the boards against water pressure, but loose enough so they can be raised or lowered by a strong hand pushing or pulling on a handgrip. Some leeboards are long and narrow; others are wide and elliptical; underwater edges should be streamlined.

THE CENTERBOARD TRUNK

If a centerboard that ordinarily works easily becomes stuck and cannot be raised or lowered, try sailing off the wind or rocking the boat while hauling on the centerboard pendant. Strong side pressure on the board when beating or reaching may make the board unresponsive. Sailing downwind releases the pressure, while rocking moves the pressure from one side to the other.

Should an object be caught between the board and the trunk, it may be freed by raising the pendant slowly and releasing it quickly several times in succession. If this does not work, probe with a wire with a hook on one end to get rid of the obstruction.

A centerboard is often jerked up sharply and violently so that the fine edges bang against the inside of the centerboard trunk. Edges are apt to chip and break. To avoid this, wedge a small piece of plastic sponge high up against the top of the inside of the trunk. It may be possible to apply a fast-drying waterproof glue to one side of the sponge and with a long stick hold the sponge in position while the glue sets. Now when the board is raised quickly, the sponge will absorb the blow.

KEEL VERSUS CENTERBOARD

The advantages of having either a centerboard or a keel are shown below.

Keel, With Ballast
- provides greater stability: a keelboat can't capsize except in extreme conditions.
- requires a certain depth of water to sail, usually about four feet for even the smallest boat.

Centerboard (or Daggerboard)
- can be raised to enter shallow water.
- can be raised for greater speeds in certain conditions.
- does not provide stability: boat can capsize.
- permits boat to be easily placed on a trailer.

Figure 16. Check the centerboard frequently for ease of operation and wear.

2
Sail Theory

The Wind

The *wind* is the most important element in sailing, and there are special words to describe the wind's changing character. The wind *veers* when it shifts in a clockwise direction (for example, south to southwest) and it *backs* counterclockwise. These variations in direction cause a sailboat to be *lifted* (permitted to head up into the wind further) if the wind change helps the boat to make her course, and *headed* if it is unfavorable to her course. The wind is described by the direction *from* which it blows: a wind out of the northeast is a northeast wind. The real direction and strength of the wind is the *true wind*, but this may not be the wind perceived aboard a boat while under way, because the true wind is combined with the boat's own speed and direction to form the *apparent wind*. Apparent wind can be quite different from true wind, and is the more important wind to consider for sail adjustment, or *trim*.

Everything that the wind passes over has a *windward* and *leeward* side. The windward side is the part of the boat, island, or other object that the wind passes over first. If you look toward the wind, you are looking to windward, or to *weather*. The *leeward* side (pronounced lōō-r-d) is the protected side of a boat. A boat may be *in the lee* of an

Figure 17. Veering or backing wind indicates a change in the wind's direction that may or may not be helpful to your boat's course.

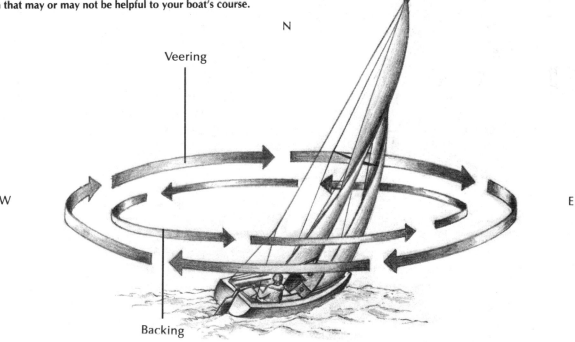

Figure 18. A carefully made suit of sails on this racing sailboat show how close in shape a sail can be to an airplane wing.

The principles underlying the theory of sailing were not too well understood until the airplane made its appearance. Intensive studies of the action of wind on wing surfaces clarified an analogy between wind and sail. The sail can be considered a wing set vertically on the hull, driving the boat by providing "lift" ahead, something like the lift upward in a plane. Sailmakers attempted to shape their sails into a section resembling a plane's wing. It became apparent that the reduction of pressure along the luff, on the forward side of the sail, was a big factor producing the drive needed to propel a hull.

Effects of the Wind

There are complex factors that bear on the aerodynamics of a sailboat working to windward, and the first thing to realize in studying the principle of why a sail drives a boat is that the wind has several different effects.

First, the wind will cause the boat to *heel over* as it hits the sails. Heeling must be kept under control; a boat needs stability to prevent her from capsizing under the pressure of wind or waves. Stability can be obtained in a hull by putting all movable weight in the boat on the high side, opposite the side the sails are on. On small boats the crew often *hikes out*—leans out over the side of the boat on the windward side, pitting their own weight against the weight of the wind on the sails.

Stability can be obtained at the design stage by putting weight low in the hull, lowering the center of gravity. If the boat has a deep keel, she will carry a casting of iron or lead bolted to the lower extremity of the keel, sometimes in the form of a bulb. This is called ballast. Hit by a puff of wind, a keelboat heels over, easily at first; but the further she heels, the greater the tendency that weight on the bottom of the keel is exerting to right the boat. Knocked down on her beam-ends, she will right herself as soon as the pressure on the sails is eased. Landsmen often marvel when they see a yacht sailing "on her ear," masts inclined at a 45-degree angle and water boiling on deck around the rail. They feel an extra puff will certainly send her

island, or of another boat, and so receive less wind. To *leeward* may refer to *downwind* (down the path of the wind); the opposite is *upwind*. A boat may change course *toward the wind* (when the bow moves upwind), or *away from the wind* (when the bow moves downwind).

Sails have been used for thousands of years to drive boats through the water, even on the simplest rafts and dugout canoes of primitive tribes. The earliest rigs were similar to a small boy's raft with a blanket sail; they had one serious limitation: they could only sail in the same direction the wind was blowing. To go to windward, these boats had to be rowed or find a favorable current to drift on.

Figure 19. A puff of wind heels the boat a bit, and the crew must shift their weight to keep her steady.

Figure 20. A casting of lead or iron in the very lowest part of the keel provides stability for this Star boat, an Olympic racer.

under. However, if she is properly designed, there are powerful forces acting to right her all the time.

The second tendency of wind is to drive the boat off sideways, to leeward. Here's something that must definitely be counteracted; otherwise a sailboat would take on the characteristics of a raft driven before the wind. A shallow-draft hull, like a rowboat, presents no vertical surface in the water to resist being driven off by lateral pressure. So a pivoted centerboard can be lowered from its trunk to prevent the boat from slipping sideways or *making leeway.* A deep-keeled vessel has a similar expanse of surface below the water to minimize leeway. The amount of lateral resistance a keel or centerboard offers is an important factor in how good a sailer the boat will be, but it is not simply a case of "more is better." The size of the keel or centerboard is a difficult decision for the designer.

Third, there is the pressure differential of the wind passing along the curved surfaces of the sails with lower pressure on the leeward side of the sails (the side away from the wind) and a buildup of higher pressure on the windward side. No sail is flat, even though it may be called flat for a particular wind condition; the sailmaker cuts and sews into each sail a certain amount of curve or fullness. This creates one side of the sail that is a concave curve and another side that is a convex curve. The wind reaches the luff of the sail and is split and altered slightly in its direction. The air that travels along the convex side of the sail, the leeward side, must travel faster in order to cover the greater distance, and in speeding up, it creates an area of lower air pressure. This difference in pressures on the two sides of a sail creates complex forces, but one of the important ones is that the sail is drawn

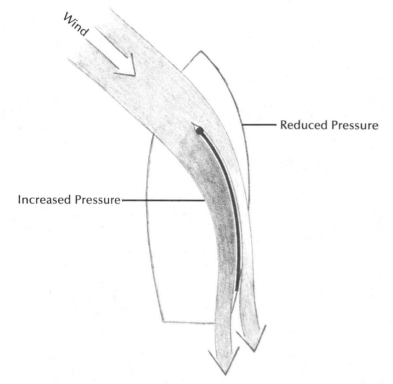

Figure 21. The reduced pressure of the wind on the leeward side of the sail creates a forward and a sideways pull on the sail.

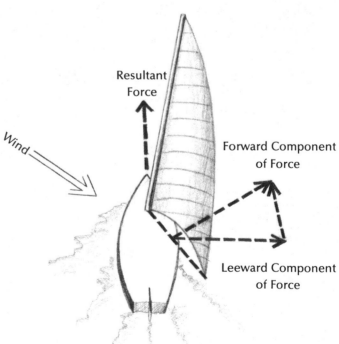

Figure 22. The sideways component is thwarted by the lateral resistance of the keel or the centerboard, and the resulting force is forward.

into the low pressure on the leeward side of the sail and moves the boat both sideways and forward. The sideways component is resisted by the centerboard or keel, and so the resulting motion of the boat is mostly forward.

The naval architect studies all these tendencies and designs a boat to minimize the features that do not contribute to propulsion of the hull, such as extra windage, and to develop the factors that do, for example, sufficient sail area. To guarantee that a maximum of propelling effect will be gained from every square foot of sail, the underwater shape of the hull is made as smooth as possible, to slip through the water with a minimum of resistance, wave making, and eddy making. For example, an underwater hull shape that tapers off to a point at the stern conforms to one of the principles of streamlining, allowing the displaced water to close in smoothly at the stern without suction, drag, or needless disturbance. Other design factors enter in, such as carrying capacity, buoyancy in the bow and stern, and stability. Such factors as the number of berths desired in the accommodations in the hull may affect design, too.

Sail Trim

The trim of each sail must be carefully controlled by the skipper or crew to get the optimum angle to the wind, and maintaining proper trim is the most important art in achieving fast, efficient sailing. Since the wind changes constantly in direction and strength, the trim must be changed constantly as well, even if only by a few inches. A good crew is constantly keeping an eye on the wind and perhaps a hand on the sheet for an adjustment that could improve the angle of the sails to the wind. See more on sail trim in Chapter 3.

Points of Sailing

A sailboat moves downwind with fairly simple aerodynamic forces—a push from behind, and is said to be *running with the wind* or *sailing free*.

Figure 23. The crew has trimmed the sails for working to windward, and the boat is doing just that. Notice the flag, and the telltales on the shroud, indicating the wind's direction.

Moving across the direction of the wind, a sailboat is *reaching*; she may be on a *broad reach*, a *beam reach*, or a *close reach*; these are the fastest points of sailing. See Figure 24.

A sailboat cannot sail directly into the wind, but sails upwind by *tacking*, which is a series of course changes, or *tacks*, that serve to work the boat in a zig-zag pattern toward her destination upwind. If the wind is coming over the port side first, the sailboat is on the *port tack*, no matter what her point of sail, and if the wind comes over her starboard side first, she is on a *starboard tack*.

There are complex aerodynamic forces involved in *working to windward*. A well-designed and well-sailed boat is said to be *weatherly*, or said to *point*

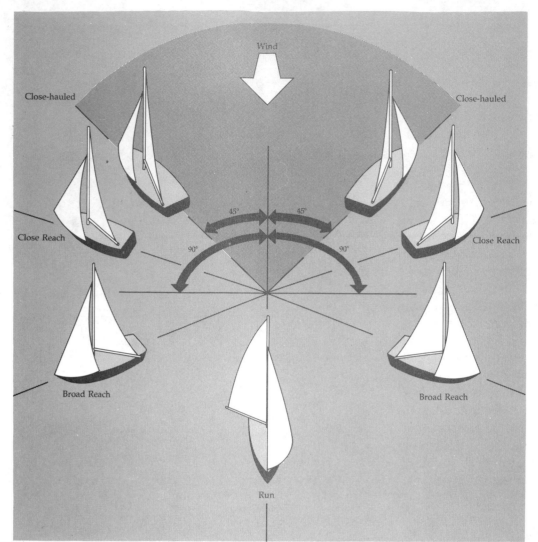

Figure 24. The relationship of the wind to the boat's course and the trim of her sails is shown here. A reach is the fastest point of sail, with the sails eased about halfway out. Close-hauled, the boat will heel more and seem to go faster. No sailboat can sail directly into the wind; most can sail no closer than about 45 degrees to the wind.

Figure 25. The four boats on the left all have clear air and are sailing nicely. Boat number 2218 cannot get clear air because of the boats to windward of her. To the right, number 6700 is far enough away so her wind is not affected by the other boats. The lines showing angle of heel help to show this.

Figure 26. The boats with clear air are moving better than number 8438 and will soon pass her.

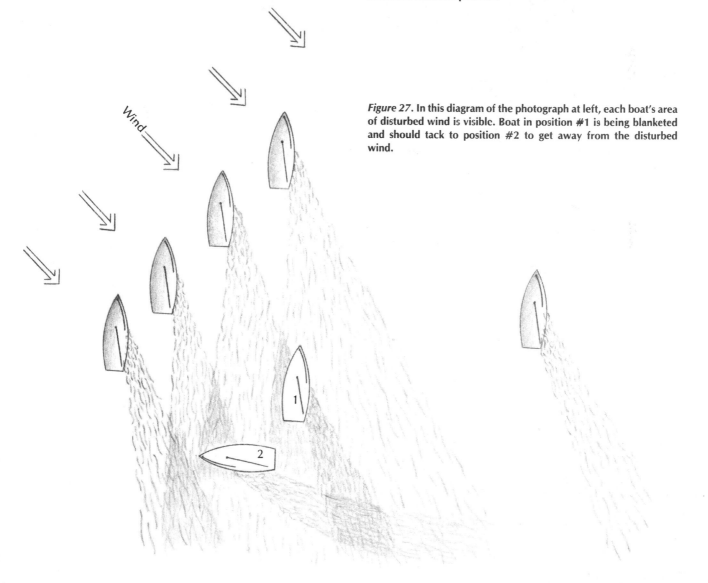

Wind

Figure 27. In this diagram of the photograph at left, each boat's area of disturbed wind is visible. Boat in position #1 is being blanketed and should tack to position #2 to get away from the disturbed wind.

1

2

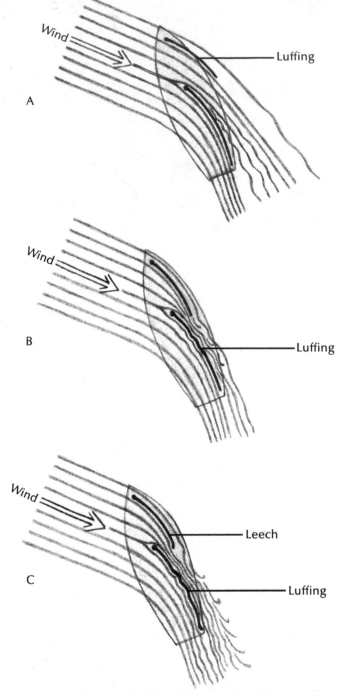

Figure 28. The trim of the jib can affect the trim of the mainsail, as shown in these diagrams. In A, the jib is too far out and efficiency is lost. In B, the jib is too far in and disturbs the mainsail. In C, a hook shape in the leech of the jib can disturb the mainsail. In all cases, a simple experimental adjustment of each sail, in or out, will show you what works best for your boat.

Figure 29. Sailing wing and wing, with the mainsail on one side and the jib on the other, is fun, but the helmsman must be careful to avoid an accidental jibe.

well, if she can sail to within 40 degrees of the direction of the wind. A boat that sails as close to the wind as possible and still maintains her speed is *beating.* She tends to *heel* noticeably on this point of sail—she leans steadily to leeward.

In going from a *close-hauled* course (close-hauled because the sails are hauled in close to the centerline of the boat) to a reach, a sailboat is said to *fall off* the wind, and the helmsman tells the crew to let the sails out, or *ease them.*

A sail is trimmed with a *sheet* to haul it in closer to the wind or ease it, whichever is best for the boat's course. A boat's sails may be *overtrimmed* for a particular wind or course if they are held in too tightly, and either the angle of the sails to the wind must be changed or the course of the boat must be adjusted to trim correctly.

If the sails are out too far or the boat is pointing

too close to the wind, the forward edges of her sails will shiver or even shake violently, and this is called *luffing*. A boat cannot sail efficiently when her sails are luffing, and she will need a change of sail trim or a change of course before she can pick up speed. If the sails are close-hauled and the boat's course is too close to the wind, she will not be able to sail well, and she will be *pinching*; the remedy is to fall off a little, steering away from the wind, or ease the sails a bit so she will sail better.

Sometimes if the boat is running before the wind, sails well out, the helmsman may decide he'll get more speed if he runs *wing and wing*, with, for instance, the mainsail out to starboard and the jib out to port. Skillful steering will be needed to keep the sails full and to avoid an accidental jibe.

The fastest point of sailing is a reach—sailing across the wind, with the sails trimmed about halfway out. A close reach is one where the boat sails close to the wind but not so close as to be "close-hauled" (see above page 26). A beam reach is a reach with the wind coming from a point directly off the beam of the boat. A broad reach is a little farther off the wind, with the wind coming from the after quarter of the boat. The reason for naming the different points of sail is so the skipper can specify which direction the boat should go by calling out the point of sail.

Figure 30. A reach, with sails out over the side of the boat, can be fast and comfortable.

3

Starting to Sail

Before raising the sails, there are a few preparations that should be made.

Remove any covers over the cockpit.

The rudder and tiller, if they are removable, should be put in place; if they are permanent, their lashings should be removed so the rudder can swing freely.

Uncleat the mainsheet and make sure it is clear for running. Release the shackle at the end of the main halyard from the boom where it is normally secured after sailing and snap it temporarily near the mast.

Lower the centerboard carefully. This provides a bit of stability in the boat as you move about.

It's a good idea to bail and sponge out any water that may have collected in the bilge.

Check that all required and recommended equipment is aboard (see Requirements, Chapter 8) and stowed carefully. This will include life preservers (PFDs), a bailer, a paddle, and an anchor and anchor rode, in even the smallest boat.

Bending on the Mainsail

Now take the mainsail out of its bag, or if it's already on the boom, take the sailcover off and untie the stops. *Stops* are the strong straps used to tie down a sail when it is furled.

Figure 31. The first thing to do when you come aboard is to roll up the cockpit cover and stow it below, and to stow any personal and safety gear.

Figure 32. Bail the boat and attach the rudder if necessary, and lower the centerboard for stability.

Figure 33. Break out the mainsail, and insert the battens if necessary. Keep the sail low in the boat so the wind doesn't catch it and whip it around.

To bend on the sail, take the foot of the sail, the edge that goes on the boom, and straighten out any kinks or twists by running your hand along its length. This lines up the slides and makes the sail easier to handle.

Slip the first slide of the clew into the track on the boom. Pull the clew along the boom, inserting the other slides in order, until the clew is almost to the end of the boom. Release the outhaul and secure it to the clew. It may attach by a pin in a car,

by a shackle, or just by a knot. At the other end of the boom, fasten the tack of the sail to the hook or pin at the gooseneck fitting. Now take up on the outhaul and secure it, so that the foot has no scallops. It should be just tight enough to keep it straight.

Now insert the battens into their respective batten pockets and tie them securely with square knots if they are the tie-in type. Usually they slide right in.

Figure 34. The foot of the sail is held by sail slides, or by a rope sewn into the edge of the sail. The outhaul adjusts the tension on the foot of the sail, and the downhaul keeps the boom from raising up too high.

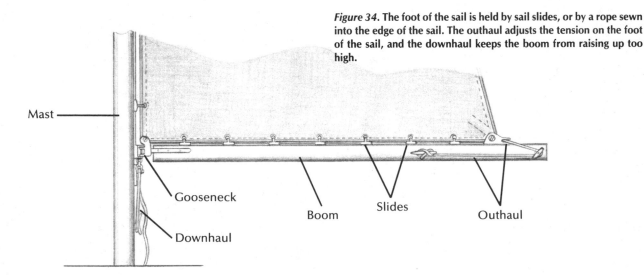

Mast

Gooseneck

Downhaul

Boom

Slides

Outhaul

Next, take the main halyard, hold it out away from the mast, and look aloft to make sure it is clear. If it has twisted around any of the stays, shrouds, or spreaders, be sure to clear it. Then shackle it to the head of the mainsail. Be sure the sail itself is not twisted.

Haul on the halyard enough to start the top sail slide into the mast track, and raise the sail enough so the slide can't drop back out. A roped edge on the sail may fit into a groove in the mast on some sails. Raise the sail, or push it up in a bundle, enough to start the next slide in the track. Continue in this manner until all the slides are in the track, then close the track with a pin if one is provided. With a crew of two, one person can insert the slides as the other raises or supports the sail. When raising the sail, it might be necessary to take a turn around a mast cleat or winch if the sail is heavy, to take the strain. On large boats a couple of turns around a winch may be necessary. However, it is often best to bend the sail on and only raise it later, when free of the dock.

Figure 36. All the slides must be in the proper order. Some sail tracks will close with a pin to prevent the slides from falling out when the sail is dropped.

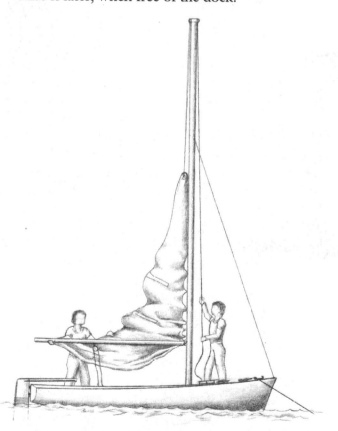

Figure 35. When ready, raise the mainsail by hauling on the main halyard. Be sure it is not twisted with the shrouds or other halyards before you raise the sail.

In most cases on small boats, the sail is raised as high as it can go without binding in the masthead sheave. For proper setting of the sail, its luff usually should be tight, with no wrinkles or scallops in the edge. If the gooseneck (the hingelike fitting on the boom) is fixed in its position—does not slide up and down on its own track—the sail must be *sweated up* on the halyard to straighten the luff. With one turn of the halyard held tight around a mast cleat, pull the halyard away from the mast at a point as high as you can reach. This raises the sail a couple of inches, which should be taken up promptly at the cleat. Repeat the process two or three times to get the luff taut. On large boats take three or four turns of the halyard on the winch, and crank the winch clockwise with the handle to raise the sail fully.

Where a sliding gooseneck fitting is used, the sail is raised as high as it will go, and the luff is stretched taut by taking up on the *downhaul*, a block and tackle under the boom that provides mechanical advantage; see Figure 34. On racing sailboats, upper and lower limits for the sail are marked by black bands on the mast.

Once the luff is taut and the halyard is cleated, you can remove the boom crotch and coil the

Figure 37. When the main has been sweated all the way up, cleat the halyard. Tension may be applied to the luff of the sail by the downhaul; it should be tight enough to keep the edge of the sail straight, but not so tight as to distort the luff of the sail.

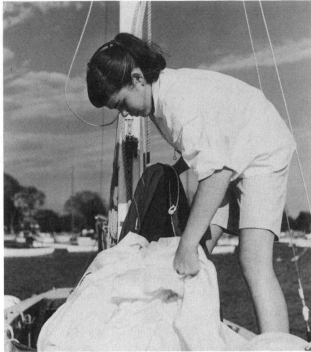

Figure 38. The first thing to do when you take the jib out of the bag is to locate the luff, which often has a wire in it, and has snaphooks along its length.

halyard fall (the now unused length of it). See page 94 for proper coiling.

If the boat is tied to a pier, the mainsheet should be slack enough so that the sail luffs completely and does not catch any wind. This keeps the boat from trying to sail away from the pier before you are ready to go.

Raising the Jib

Attach the tack (lowest, forward corner) of the jib to the deck fitting at the bow, and attach two sheets to the jib's clew with a bowline (see Chapter 7) or a snap hook. Lead the sheets outside the shrouds and back to their block or their cleat in the cockpit. Shackle the jib halyard to the head of the sail, after making sure that the luff is not twisted and that the halyard itself is clear aloft. *Hank on* the snap hooks to the forestay in sequence, being careful not to twist them. If all else is ready to go, you can raise the jib now and start

off, but it is often wise to leave the pier, the mooring, or the beach with the jib tied down on the foredeck and raise it only when you are clear of other boats. It makes a simpler, more controlled departure.

When you do raise the jib, be sure to apply enough tension on the halyard that the jib's luff (leading edge) does not make loose scallops but looks as straight as the line of the forestay itself, even when under wind pressure. This may require considerable weight or "sweating up" to achieve the proper tension, as above. A jib halyard winch can be helpful here. While the halyard is being set up, the jib sheets should be allowed to run free so that no wind fills the sail, making the job tougher. Once secured, coil the halyard below the cleat and hang up the coil as shown. As mentioned before, the sheet lead, the angle of pull the sheet exerts on the sail, is very important to the proper shape of the jib and should be adjusted if necessary. This can be done while under sail and tried out in several different locations. In general the lead should make the sail an even airfoil shape, with

Figure 39. Attach the snaphooks to the forestay, making sure they are in the correct order and are not twisted. Attach two jib sheets to the clew of the sail.

Figure 40. When the tack is fastened to the base of the forestay, and the halyard fastened to the head of the sail, the jib is ready to hoist.

Helpful Hints

ROLLER-FURLING JIBS

Many boats today, particularly larger cruising boats, have a special jib that can be set, trimmed, and furled by lines that lead to the cockpit. The jib is attached at its leading edge to a revolving rod that replaces or augments the forestay. The jib can be rolled around this rod headstay much like a roll-up window blind and furled completely without touching the deck. This is a very handy method of handling large, cumbersome jibs. It permits setting the jib by merely hauling on the sheet while releasing the furling line on the furling drum. When the time comes to furl again, the sheet is eased, and the sail is rolled up by the furling line. Care must be taken that the sail, while rolled, is protected from the ultraviolet rays of the sun by a layer of sacrificial material, often blue fabric, at the exposed edge.

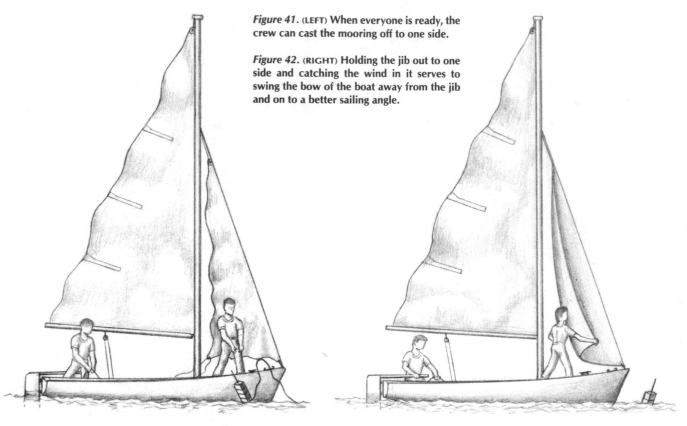

Figure 41. (LEFT) When everyone is ready, the crew can cast the mooring off to one side.

Figure 42. (RIGHT) Holding the jib out to one side and catching the wind in it serves to swing the bow of the boat away from the jib and on to a better sailing angle.

curves somewhat parallel to the curves of the mainsail nearby. Neither the leech nor the foot (see the Mainsail, Figure 9) should be stretched too tight.

Winches are necessary in larger boats to handle the large loads of the sail, and they make it possible to adjust the sail even under tremendous pressure. Winches turn in only one direction, usually clockwise (the same direction no matter which side of the boat they're placed on). They usually have a removable crank-type handle which gives you a mechanical advantage and can ratchet backward freely. This handle should be removed and stowed nearby whenever someone's hand is not directly on it, or else you run the risk of knocking it overboard. When using a winch, be careful that fingers and long hair do not get caught up in the lines under tension.

Leaving a Mooring

When you are ready to cast off the mooring, decide the direction in which you want to sail, taking note of other boats, docks, or shoals, and

Figure 43. If you have an engine, be careful to leave the mooring to one side, well away from the spinning propeller blades.

the wind. If sails are already up, as above, then hold the jib *aback* by holding its clew out *opposite* to the direction you want the bow to swing when you release the mooring. The wind will catch the jib and turn the bow; when both sails fill, let go the jib and haul in the jib sheet and the mainsheet.

Pull in both sails to their best angle to the wind. See below for details on sail trim and points of sail.

It may be necessary to let the boat drift back a short distance before putting the sails aback, so the boat will not hit her mooring buoy when she begins to move ahead.

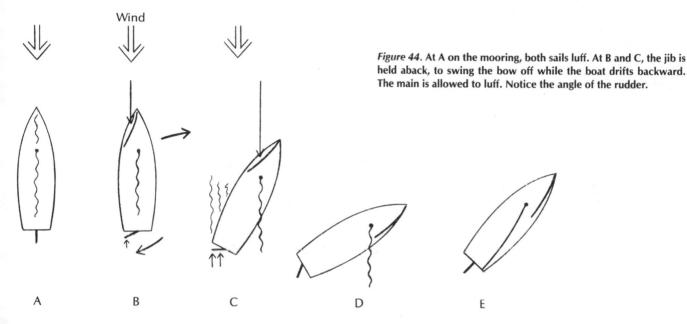

Figure 44. At A on the mooring, both sails luff. At B and C, the jib is held aback, to swing the bow off while the boat drifts backward. The main is allowed to luff. Notice the angle of the rudder.

A   B   C   D   E

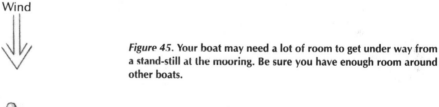

Figure 45. Your boat may need a lot of room to get under way from a stand-still at the mooring. Be sure you have enough room around other boats.

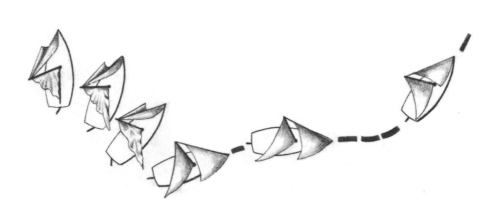

Telltales

At a mooring, it is usually easy to tell which way the wind is blowing. The boat's bow will naturally point into the wind. However, if there is little or no wind or a very strong current, the boat may not point so accurately into the wind. *Telltales*—bits of yarn tied to the shrouds, flags on board, or even an electronic sensor at the masthead—all will indicate where the wind is coming from. Every boat should have a telltale of some kind, no matter how large or small. The telltale is the most important indicator of the wind's direction and the boat's relationship to the wind, and it is the key to good sail trim and good boat speed.

Telltales will flutter in a particular direction across the boat for each point of sail, indicated in the diagram. Every boat's telltales will have a little bit different angle for her ideal trim, and to know this for every point of sail is a mark of getting to know your boat well.

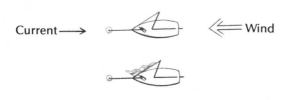

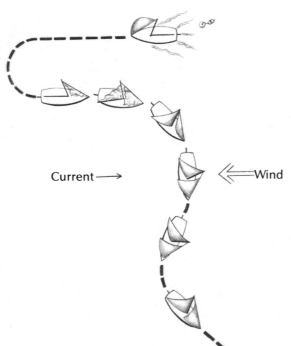

Helpful Hints

TELLTALES IN THE SAIL

Small telltales, sewn into the fabric of the jib, can be very useful in achieving perfect trim on the sail. By sewing an eight-to-ten-inch yarn through the sail, in a location about one foot back from the jib luff and halfway up the jib, you have a tiny telltale on each side of the sail, about four to five inches long on each side. When both yarns are flowing smoothly in parallel, the trim of the sail is good. Should one or the other of the yarns begin to shoot up or flutter wildly, trim is either too tight or too loose. The inner (windward) yarn fluttering indicates the boat is pinched, too close to the wind for maximum effectiveness. You must either head the boat downwind a bit or bring in the sail. The outer yarn (leeward) fluttering indicates the sail should be eased or the boat's course altered upwind a little bit to restore the smooth flow of air across the sail.

If not already installed in your sails, a telltale is the simplest and easiest addition you can make for better boat handling. Some racing boats carry several sets of these telltales, festooned along the length of the luff.

Figure 46. **If there is a strong current to keep the boat from heading into the wind, it might be advantageous to raise the jib and start right off from the mooring, raising the mainsail later.**

Figure 47. Beware of the swinging boom when raising the mainsail. The boat should be pointed directly into the wind so the sails luff amidships.

Figure 48. With the sails up and drawing, the boat seems to come alive.

Under Way

After leaving the mooring, you are under sail with both main and jib up and ready to practice some boat-handling skills. While steering a fairly straight course, you should begin by adjusting sail trim. Let out one sheet until the sail luffs (shakes vigorously). With the sail completely luffing, the boat will not move well and probably will not heel very much. As you slowly bring in the sheet, you will see several things happen: the sail will begin to *fill* with wind and take on an airfoil shape, the boat may begin to heel over slightly under pressure from the wind, and the boat's speed will increase. Continue to bring the sail in until all traces of luffing disappear. Usually the last visible luffing will be along the leading edge of the sail (hence the name luff given to that area of the sail). When the sail is trimmed in just to the point of not luffing and not far beyond that point, it is correctly trimmed. Mainsail and jib should each be trimmed in this manner and must be retrimmed at every course change and every wind change. Proper sail trim requires constant attention and should not be ignored.

Exceptions to this method of trimming occur when the boat is pointed so close to the direction the wind is from that the sails cannot be brought in any further and they are still luffing. The simple remedy for this is to steer the boat away from the wind a few degrees (move the tiller slightly away from the sails).

Sail trim can be difficult to determine also when the boat is going downwind and the sails are way out over the side of the boat. Then another method of sail trim can be used, usually with telltales.

The best test of trim is simply to sail alongside another similar boat, adjust trim, and see if your boat moves ahead or drops astern. There may be other factors affecting speed, of course; this is what yacht racing is all about, and it's the best way to learn about proper trim.

Coming About

Your initial course may be any one of the points of sailing discussed earlier, close-hauled, reaching, or running, but eventually you will have to change course and bring the wind onto the other side of the sails. *Tacking* and *jibing* are the two means used to accomplish this. In tacking, the bow of the boat

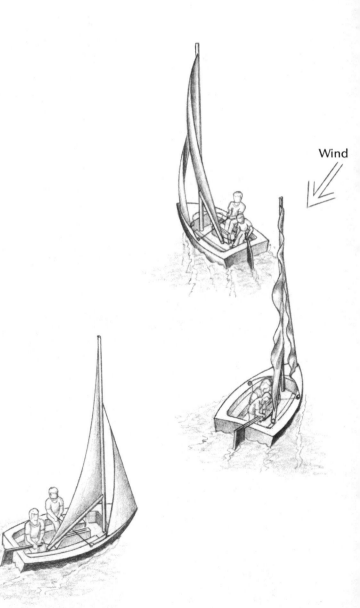

Wind

Figure 49. **To come about, the helmsman starts by moving the tiller toward the sails. The sails begin to luff and the crew changes sides while releasing the jib. The helmsman straightens the tiller while the crew brings in the jib on the new side.**

goes through the wind, and the sails are close-hauled first on one tack, then on the other. A succession of tacks is usually necessary to make progress toward a destination to windward. *Coming about* is a term used for tacking.

Coming about is easy. From a close-hauled course, steer the boat toward the direction from which the wind is coming and continue around until the sails fill on the other side. Since a boat preparing to tack is usually sailing at an angle of about 45 degrees off the wind and will be at the same angle to the wind after the tack is executed, the complete turn is about 90 degrees. In other words, you will be heading toward a point that was directly abeam before starting to tack.

To illustrate the maneuver, suppose you are sailing close-hauled. The helmsman gives the command "Ready about." This warns the crew that they should be ready to handle the jib sheets and ready to move to the opposite side of the boat.

The command "Hard-a-lee" means the helmsman is pushing the tiller toward the boom, over to the lee side of the boat, away from the wind. The bow swings into the wind, and as the jib starts to flutter, a crew member should release the jib. Both sails luff, then swing to the opposite side of the boat as the boat continues her turn. The mainsail again fills with wind, and the jib sheet on the new leeward side of the boat must be hauled in to trim the jib. As the boat makes the turn, the crew must move across the boat and take places on the new windward side as the boat heels on the new tack. The tiller is brought back to center and the boat is steered to the new course.

When the boat is sailing with the wind coming from the starboard side, it is on the *starboard tack*. When the wind is coming from the port side, it is on the *port tack*. These are important considerations in right-of-way and racing situations.

In tacking, letting the jib sheet fly allows the boat to swing more easily. However, it should be released only after the jib starts to flutter—perhaps a moment or two after the tiller has been moved—to maintain drive in the sail as long as possible. Normally there is no adjustment to the mainsheet during a tack. If the boat goes onto a reach after the tack, the mainsheet should be eased as the boat bears off onto the new course.

Figure 50. In racing, boats tack back and forth, trying to cross each other and get to the mark first. Right-of-way rules are important here.

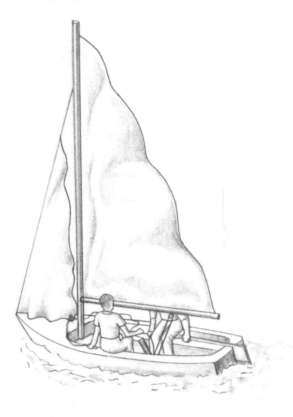

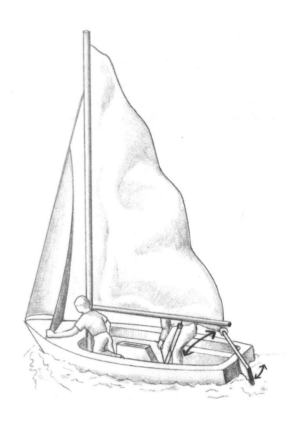

Figure 51. To get out of irons, pull the jib out to one side and the tiller to the other side. The boat will back away from the side the jib is on.

Wind

Figure 52. To get out of irons in a single-sail boat, push the mainsail and the tiller to the same side and the boat will turn in that direction.

How a boat is trimmed may affect her balance and turning movement; for example, if there is too much weight forward, the bow may bury itself in the sea and hinder the boat's ability to turn. If there is too much weight in the stern, causing the bow to lift slightly from the water, the wind may catch the bow and keep the boat from turning.

If the boat fails to complete the turn and the bow points directly into the wind, the boat is said to be *in irons* and she will not sail. To get out of irons, follow the same procedure used for leaving a mooring. Hold the jib aback on the side away from the direction you want to steer; you can also put the rudder *opposite* this direction.

To avoid getting into irons, keep momentum as the boat comes around. Sometimes the tiller has to be snapped over, in light air, and other times brought around easily with a long shoot into the wind, in good sailing breezes. Generally a boat should come about easily with good momentum so that she will actually shoot up into the wind before falling off onto the new tack.

If the wind is so light that the boat cannot come around on her own momentum, she may need a bit of coaxing. Slack the sheets and resort to a bit of *sculling*. Sculling involves a vigorous swinging of the tiller (and the rudder) back and forth; it gives some slight forward motion to the boat, and in most cases it will provide enough momentum to complete the maneuver. Sculling is not permitted in racing. The tiller should never be slammed over to an extreme angle, because the rudder may act as a brake and stop the boat's forward motion.

When coming about in big seas, a boat *loses way* quickly and is slowed by the force of the waves. Keep good speed on the boat and choose the smoother, smaller rollers to maneuver in.

Tacking

In order for a sailboat to get to a destination upwind, she must sail a zig-zag course. Each zig or zag (tack) is sailed as close to the wind as possible; this is about 45 degrees from the true wind and 90 degrees from the previous tack. You sail close-hauled, first on one tack, come about, then sail on the other tack, come about, and keep tacking until you reach the destination.

It is usually important to know where the boat will be heading when she completes the tack. You must be sure of clearing other boats and of *fetching the mark* or point of land you want to round. This should be calculated by the helmsman before the tack begins and will affect the timing of the tack. You should look directly abeam, over the windward side, just about straight out from the side of the boat. On the compass, the new course after the tack will be about 90 degrees from your present course.

Of course you must adjust the tacking angle for the performance characteristics of your boat; some boats are more *weatherly,* sail closer to the wind, and can tack before the 90-degree angle is reached; others will not come as close as 45 degrees to the wind and must wait until the angle is greater than 90 degrees before tacking. Again you must experiment and learn about your own boat.

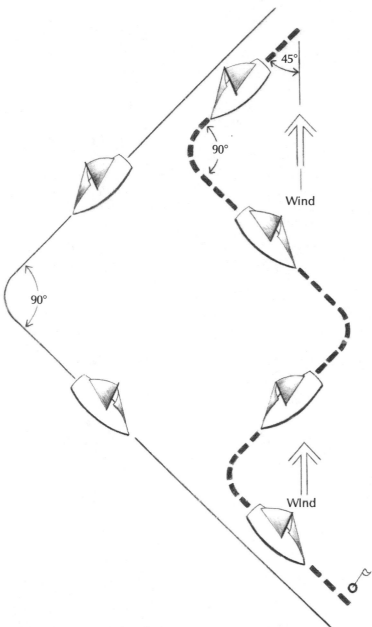

Figure 53. Tacking usually involves a course change of 90 degrees. Often long tacks will get you upwind faster than numerous shorter tacks.

Jibing

Jibing is another method of bringing the wind to the opposite side of the sails. In jibing, the stern, rather than the bow, of the boat crosses the wind. Because of some inherent dangers relating to the momentum of the boom, this maneuver should be executed by the beginner only in light to moderate winds. In a hard blow, the safest way to get onto the other tack may be to come about, described earlier.

Generally you jibe when you want to change your course when sailing before the wind or when the wind has shifted. A jibe may be used when you have to round a buoy or breakwater.

Here is how a controlled jibe is done (gibe and gybe are alternate spellings for the same thing): You are sailing before the wind or on a broad reach with the boom way out over the side of the boat. Begin the maneuver by dropping the centerboard halfway down, then haul in on the mainsheet, heading gradually farther downwind the whole time.

Keep hauling on the mainsheet until the boom is over the cockpit. Be sure to keep the mainsheet clear so that it can run out without snarling; let the coils of the sheet drop loosely.

Steer carefully and slowly, push the tiller away from the side the boom is on. The wind will get in back of the mainsail and will snap the boom over fast; keep your head low, shift weight to the opposite side, and don't let the mainsheet sweep into anything or anyone. To ease the jolt, let the mainsheet run out, but control its run so that the boom will not slam into the shrouds. Keep on course as much as possible, bring in the jib sheet on the new tack so that the jib again draws, and you are on your way again.

Remember to always shorten the mainsheet before a jibe. Do not allow the boom to swing freely from one side to the other except in the very, very lightest breeze. In these cases, where there is no strain on the mast or rigging, the boom is often pushed by hand from one side to the other. In

Figure 54. In jibing, the boom swings all the way across as the boat changes course downwind. Watch your head in this maneuver, and keep the boom under control with the mainsheet.

Figure 55. In coming about, the boom swings only a few feet and usually does not require adjustment as the boat changes course 90 degrees upwind.

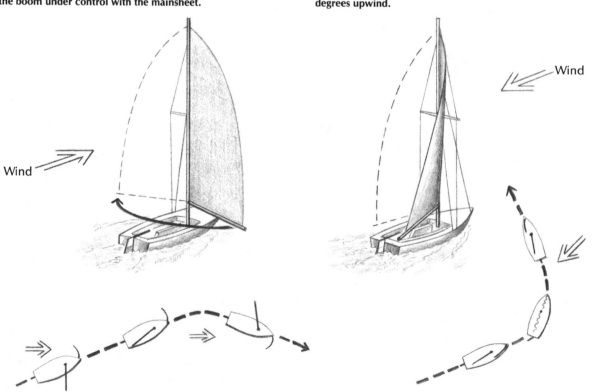

Figure 56. The mainsail is brought all the way in before the course is changed for a jibe. When the wind catches the new side of the sail, the sheet is allowed to run out under control.

Figure 57, where the boat is altering course to round a breakwater, the boat jibes from a broad reach on one tack to a broad reach on the other tack. On both tacks the wind is on the quarter, and the jib is not blanketed by the mainsail.

An *accidental jibe* can occur whenever the wind is allowed to catch the mainsail on the lee side and swing it violently across the boat to the other side. It usually is the result of inattentive helmsmanship. The boat has been allowed to sail "beyond" dead downwind. Because it can be dangerous to crewmen's heads and to the rigging and can bring on a capsize, it can and should be avoided by not sailing too close to dead downwind.

Note in Figure 58 that with the wind almost astern, the jib is set on the side opposite the

Wind

Figure 57. To round a breakwater or a buoy, a jibe from reach to reach is often useful. Note that the mainsheet is still brought in before any course change is made.

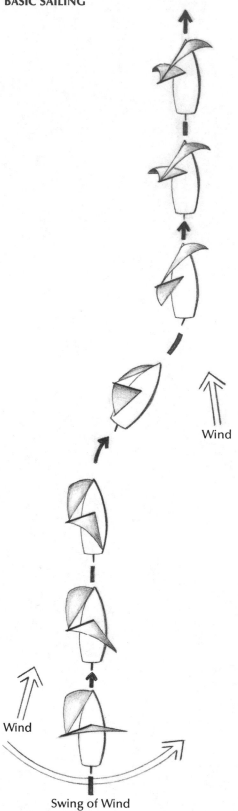

Wind

Wind

Swing of Wind

Figure 58. Jibing may involve only a very small course change, particularly when done with a favorable wind shift. Always be cautious when running in seas or shifting winds.

mainsail. This is sailing *wing and wing.* If the jib were on the same side as the mainsail, it might be blanketed and ineffectual.

A boat can also be tacked downwind in a zig-zag, a maneuver that is particularly useful when the wind is not steady but repeatedly shifts a few degrees left or right from directly astern. It is also done when the wind is strong and waves high, to avoid the possibility of an accidental jibe.

Reaching is generally the fastest point of sailing, and some racing skippers may also reach, jibe, and reach on a downwind course rather than sail directly before the wind. However, they must consider the time involved in making the jibe and the ground lost in the turn as well as the added distance covered on the zig-zag course.

Whoosh!

Figure 59. An accidental jibe can be dangerous and frightening. Careful attention to the tiller and the wind direction can prevent it. If in doubt, bring the sails in a bit and sail on a broad reach instead of running.

Using the Centerboard

There are no hard rules for handling centerboards. It is not necessary for the centerboard to be down at all times. Different skippers use the centerboard in different ways under similar conditions. Weight and placement of the crew, point of sailing, hull form, and helm response all govern the centerboard's position.

In general, a lowered board aids steering, helps in keeping a boat from rolling in a seaway, and reduces leeway; but it adversely affects speed through the water. When the boat is sailing to windward, the centerboard should be lowered all the way down for maximum lateral resistance. When the boat is running, the board is all the way up to reduce drag. For reaching, the board is raised to positions between these two extremes, with more board down when sailing on a close reach than when broad off the wind.

The board should be down when beating or close-reaching, for here the reduction of leeway is more important than speed through the water.

The board is kept all the way up when sailing before the wind in smooth water. Lowering the

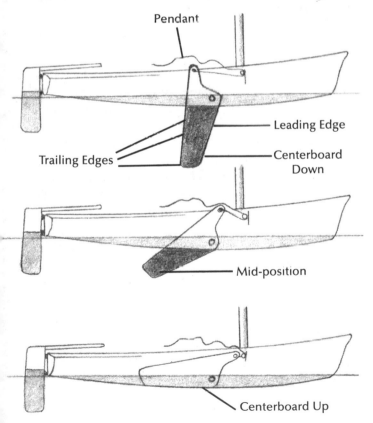

Pendant

Leading Edge

Centerboard Down

Trailing Edges

Mid-position

Centerboard Up

board slightly will help steering and will reduce weaving or rolling in rough going. Assuming the boat is kept *on her feet,* leeway and angle of heel are not important in this point of sailing because all forces are working to drive the boat in one direction, downwind.

Skillful racing skippers adjust the centerboard almost as much as their sails as they strive for balance between trim, crew position, helm, and centerboard to get the best performance from the boat.

Controlling the Angle of Heel

While a small boat's hull shape adds to stability, the angle of the *heel* is controlled mostly by the crew. Crew members move across the boat, inboard and outboard, to counterbalance the heeling caused by the wind. Except in extremely strong winds, when wind has to be spilled from the sails for safety, the methods described here are most effective in keeping a boat sailing at the proper angle of heel for maximum speed.

Any boat, whether keel or centerboard, should not be allowed to heel more than approximately 20 degrees because the hull shape, at this angle and greater, offers too much resistance to the water, and the boat slows down. It's a good idea to keep the lee rail from going under too often.

If the crew, by *hiking out*—leaning outboard from the rail—cannot correct or reduce this excessive angle of heel, reduce sail or spill wind from the sails. When sailing under extreme conditions, a boat will move faster under shortened sail with less heel. Besides slowing the boat, excessive heel imposes severe strains on rigging, sails, and crew. See the section on reefing in Chapter 5.

In light air, when the wind is too feeble to heel the vessel, the boat may be purposely tipped to leeward by moving the crew to the leeward side. The sails will then assume a natural curve and cause whatever air there is to flow easily over

Figure 60. **The centerboard can be adjusted for different points of sail: all the way down for close-hauled sailing when the most lateral resistance is needed; halfway up for reaching; and all the way up for running with the wind.**

A

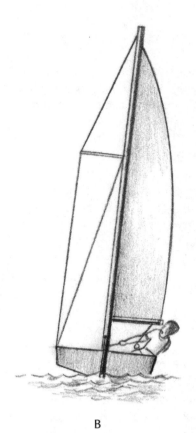

B

Figure 61. **Hiking out can add stability to a small boat and help her sail faster. It also requires strength and stamina if you hike out for long.**

Figure 62. **In very light air, weight on the leeward side of the boat can help to fill the sails and keep the boat moving.**

them. In a fleet of boats sailing in light airs, those which keep the proper curvature in their sails move faster.

In gentle and medium winds the angle of heel is also easily controlled and does not present much of a problem. The crew moves slightly to the windward side to balance the boat. The crew should keep as low as possible to reduce wind resistance and should not jump around. The movements on board should be easy and smooth, with no jarring or bumping.

In strong winds the crew tries to keep the boat upright and sailing fast at as small an angle of heel as possible. The crew sits up on the high (windward) side. The more the boat heels, the farther out the crew leans. Straps running along the side of the centerboard trunk, called *hiking* or *toe straps*, furnish the toehold needed to keep the crew from falling overboard.

When properly done, hiking is most effective for reducing the angle of heel. The crew must be agile and quick to sense any change in wind strength, for it is just as necessary to sit upright when a puff lets up as it is to lean out when the gust strikes.

On larger keelboats or in those sailing classes that do not permit hiking straps, lying along the weather rail with a firm grip is the most effective method of flattening the boat before having to reduce sail.

Figure 63. Almost completely out of the boat, these Laser sailors use tiller extensions and hiking straps to help them balance the boat in strong winds.

4

Mooring and Anchoring

After you have learned to hold a boat on course on the various points of sailing and to tack and jibe in normal conditions, you need to know how to bring the boat back up to the mooring, or to an anchorage. *Mooring*, tying the boat to a buoy which is chained to a weight on the bottom, will be discussed first.

Mooring

In all approaches to a mooring buoy, the idea is to bring the boat downwind of it, then to shoot up into the wind to a stop alongside of it. Then merely lean over, pick up the *pendant* attached to the buoy, and make it fast to the mooring cleat without strain or fuss.

In ordinary sailing breezes, most skippers learn to do this easily and without mishap. The trick is to learn when to shoot up (head directly) into the wind and how far away the boat should be from the mooring when the luff is started.

The distance, measured in boat lengths, needed to reach a stop by the mooring buoy depends on the strength of the wind and boat type. Since most small centerboard boats do not have much forward momentum when coming up into the wind, a distance of only one or two boat lengths in light air, or three in heavier winds, should be allowed. Different boats, of course, may require different distances, depending on hull form and displacement. See Figures 64–67.

Figure 64. To pick up a mooring, the boat should be aimed for a point several boat lengths straight downwind of the mooring. For a light centerboard boat this might be only two boat lengths below the mooring. For a heavier keelboat it might be four boat lengths below the mooring.

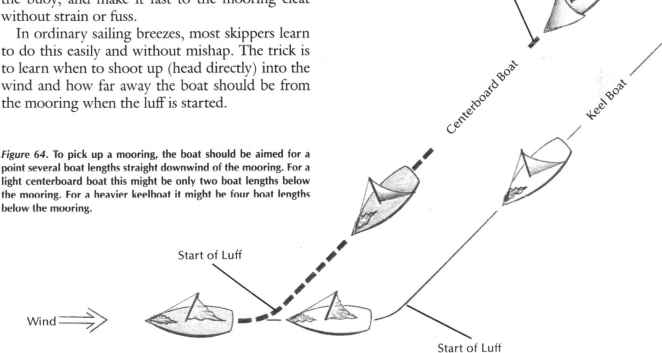

51

Keelboats maintain more *way on* (momentum) when coming into the wind; therefore more distance to the buoy from the luffing point must be allowed. This may be as many as six boat lengths or as few as three. The best way to find out is to make several attempts, and only on the closest, slowest approach should you actually pick up the buoy.

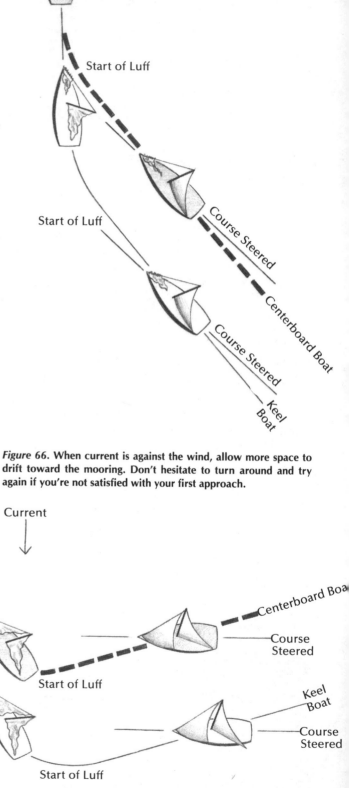

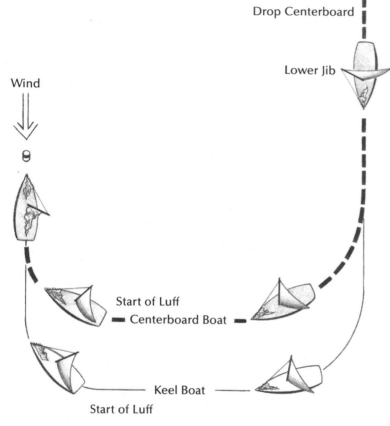

Figure 65. Dropping the centerboard and lowering the jib helps in stability and control before approaching the mooring. Remember to give yourself plenty of time to slow the boat down before trying to pick up the mooring.

Figure 66. When current is against the wind, allow more space to drift toward the mooring. Don't hesitate to turn around and try again if you're not satisfied with your first approach.

Figure 67. Against a strong current and against the wind, the boat's speed will drop quickly when you luff the sails, and fewer boat lengths will be needed for time to kill the boat's speed.

Figure 68. When motoring up to the mooring, approach slowly, and be sure you don't overrun the pendant and foul the propeller blades. A boathook may be necessary if the boat has high sides.

With a centerboard boat, drop the board all the way down before starting to luff. This gives the boat more stability and helps steering.

On most boats you should leave the jib up for maneuverability; it can be lowered right after the mooring pendant is secured.

In strong winds and currents, picking up the mooring is not so easy. Distance and speed are more critical, and thorough planning is necessary to pick up the mooring in a seamanlike manner. Skippers may miss several times before making a mooring, and it is better to try again than to try to pick it up when the boat is moving too fast.

Dousing Sails

Once the mooring line has been secured (be sure it passes through the bow chock), the jib and mainsail can be lowered promptly.

First put the boom crotch in place and set the boom into the notch. This keeps the boom from swinging and getting in the way, particularly on a windy day. Some boats will have a *topping lift* to hold up the boom.

Now uncleat the main halyard, but be careful in handling the coil. It must not be thrown aside any old way, but should be cleared for running by being placed neatly right side up, so that the halyard leads from the top and will run out without snarling. With one hand controlling the halyard, you should allow the sail to come down smartly. Use the other hand to pull the sail down

Figure 69. Sails should be doused soon after picking up the mooring. Be sure to support the boom with a boom crotch or a topping lift so that it won't come down on someone's head.

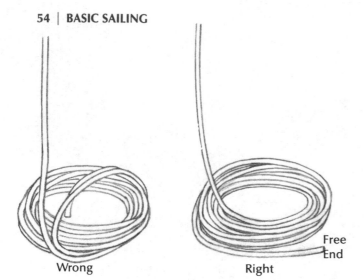

Wrong   Right

Free End

Figure 70. In preparing to drop a sail, lay the halyard on the deck and be sure the line pays out from the top of the coil, not the bottom. Otherwise, knots may form and the whole coil may fly up in the air.

or to guide the folds over the boom. Take care not to let any of the sail go overboard.

Sometimes in a strong wind, because of the violent flapping of the sail, slides may stick in the mast track and stop the descent of the sail. A few sharp tugs on the luff should free it.

After the sail is down, cleat the loose end of the halyard. Never allow the halyard to hang free; it may run up the mast and leave you with the sticky job of recovery at the top of the mast.

Take the battens out of the sail and tie them together. Stow them carefully in a spot where they can't be stepped on, broken, or kicked overboard. Now unshackle the halyard from the head of the sail and secure it to a lifeline or part of the boom to prevent the halyard from running up the mast and through the masthead sheave. Release the tack from the gooseneck and the clew from the out-haul. Whether the sail is removed from the boom and taken off the boat or left *furled* (see below) and under a sailcover will depend on the type of boat and the habits of the skipper.

While it does not harm a dacron sail to be stowed wet, it is a good practice to bundle a wet sail loosely and carry it ashore, where you can hang it to dry and fold it properly.

Fasten the halyard to the gooseneck or outhaul, whichever you prefer. Either place is ok, but some skippers prefer the outhaul in case the boom should jump out of the crotch, as can happen in

rough weather. Then the halyard would hold the boom high and prevent damage to the deck or boom. Take the slack out of the halyard and make it fast. Coil what is left and secure it on the cleat and coil the mainsheet.

Unship the rudder and daggerboard, if these are the removable type, and fasten them down in the cockpit so they can't slide around. Make fast all loose gear and coil all lines neatly and evenly. Sponge out the bilge and clean the topsides and deck. If there is any fresh water on board, maybe in an ice chest, use this to wipe off varnished surfaces to remove saltwater residue. Raise the centerboard all the way to protect if from excessive swinging and banging. Unroll the cockpit cover and fasten it in place. Then you are ready to go ashore. Note that shooting into the wind for a landing at a pier or float involves the same sailing procedures as shooting a mooring—plus the need to fend off. If you have an engine to assist in

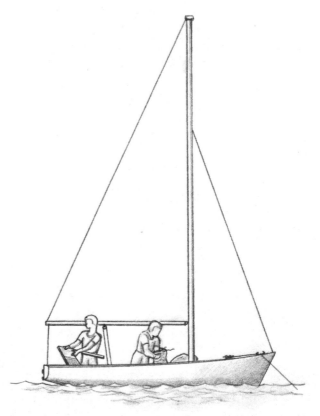

Figure 71. Unship the rudder, bag the sails, secure all halyards and sheets, and put cockpit covers and sail covers on before leaving the boat.

making a landing, just remember to come in at dead slow and be sure no one's hand or feet get between the boat and the pier.

Furling the Mainsail

On larger boats where the sails are large and heavy, furling the main on the boom is a common practice. It must be protected by a sailcover when left for any time to protect it from the ultraviolet rays of the sun.

Occasionally a small sailboat must be left temporarily unattended where it is not practical to un-bend the sails and stow them in their bags. In these circumstances, a good sailor will furl them neatly. *Furling* is a seamanlike way of securing sails and keeping them from flogging themselves to tatters in a breeze.

There are four steps to a good furl. First, insert the long narrow ties, called *stops*, between the

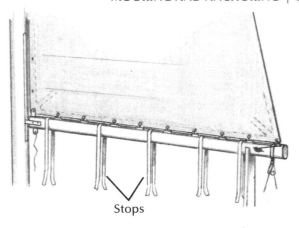

Figure 73. Four or five sail stops should be placed between the boom and the sail before the mainsail is lowered.

boom and the sail. Second, lower the mainsail. Third, furl the sail in smooth folds. And fourth, secure it with the previously inserted stops.

Note that before the sail is lowered, the stops are tucked *between the sail and sail track*, as shown in Figure 73. Sometimes a loose half hitch is used to hold them in place. One stop is placed close to the gooseneck and another forward of the outhaul. Others are spaced evenly in between. The number of stops depends on the length of the boom; on a sailboat of 20 feet or less, four will be enough.

After all the stops are in place, the main is lowered. The folds of the sail are neatly arranged, then pulled or stretched aft to remove any wrinkles

Figure 72. Many large boats leave the mainsail on the boom all season. It must be neatly furled and covered with a sail cover when not in use.

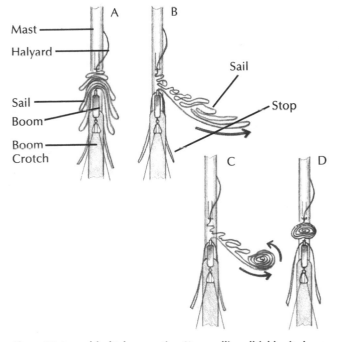

Figure 74. A good furl takes practice. Keep pulling all folds aft along the boom. Fold the whole sail into one final fold that covers the sail, then roll it onto the top of the boom.

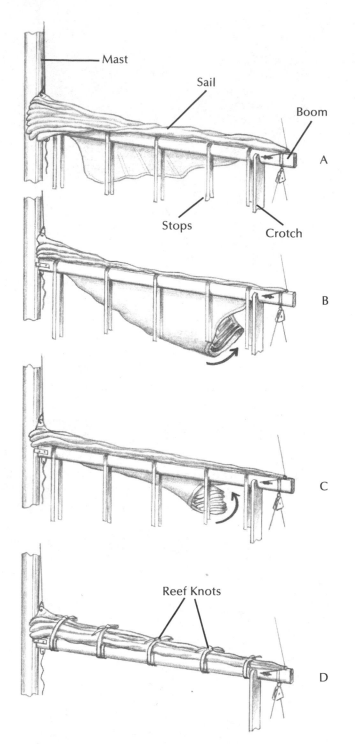

or unevenness in the folds. Battens are usually removed unless the boat is to be used again that day. When battens are left in their pockets, see that they lie parallel to the boom; otherwise they may be broken.

Now all of the sail is pulled to one side of the boom and allowed to lie on the bottommost, and largest, fold. This fold should be pulled out to receive all the following folds. Then the sail is tightly rolled, neatly and evenly, with the bottom fold always on the outside. To prevent bunching of the folds, remember to pull aft on them as they are rolled. The sail is rolled until it comes to rest on top of the sail track. It is held there firmly by the stops and not allowed to slip to either side of the boom.

Finally, the ends of the stops are brought up and crossed *over* the rolled sails (Figure 76B) and pulled tight, then passed and crossed *under the boom* and again pulled tight (Figure 76C). Again the ends are brought up to the top of the roll and firmly tied with either a square knot or a slippery reef knot (see Chapter 7).

Tension is kept on the stops as they are passed around the rolled sail and boom to prevent the sail from losing its roll.

A good seaman of the old school could furl and stop a sail so tightly that hard-driving rain or moisture could hardly penetrate its folds.

Figure 75. At A, the entire sail is pulled over to one side of the boom. All material should be pulled aft from the mast to smooth out wrinkles. At B and C, the sail is folded into the outermost fold. At D, the furl is tied on top of the boom with sail stops.

Figure 76. The furled sail is held by stops placed between the sail and the boom. Note how the stop goes twice around the sail to hold it in a roll and to hold it on top of the boom. Finish with a reef knot, shown in Chapter 7.

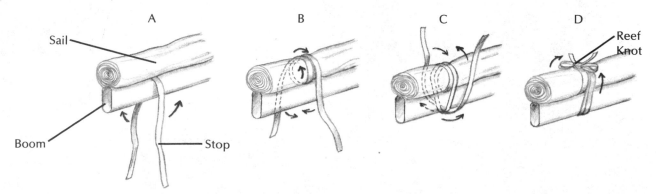

Anchoring Under Sail

There are many factors involved in anchoring a boat. Seamanlike procedures and intelligent use of good equipment will make the boat safe and secure.

On approaching an anchorage, the first thing to do is to scan the harbor for the best place to anchor. Sail back and forth, if necessary, to locate a spot that is out of the prevailing and anticipated wind and sheltered from troublesome waves. Generally there is very little trouble finding such a site for a small boat. Because of shoal draft, small boats can anchor readily in waters that are much too shallow for larger vessels. Allowance must be made for the rise and fall of tide.

If the anchorage is crowded, look for a spot among boats of your own boat's general size and one that is at least three or four boat lengths away from the nearest boat, whether she is ahead, astern, or on either beam. This allowance gives you ample swinging area should the wind change or the tide turn. If you anchor among larger boats, allowances must be made for their greater swinging radius.

Bring out the anchor and its line, called the rode, and if not already fastened together, tie with the knot called the anchor bend (see Chapter 7). A permanently made up anchor rode might be shackled to the anchor. Take the anchor and line, along with a *sounding lead* (or some other means of determining water depth), to the foredeck.

Figure 77. With her anchor and rode neatly coiled on the foredeck, this sloop might be bound for distant harbors.

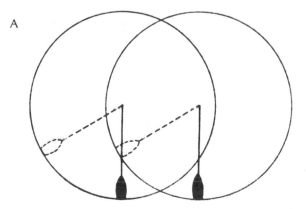

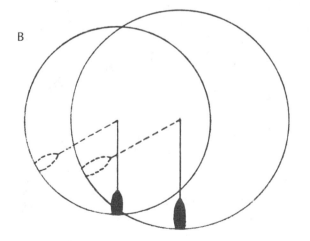

Figure 78. Larger boats will require more room than smaller boats, and may respond differently to different wind and current conditions. Note how the larger boat, in B, could easily swing and interfere with the smaller boat.

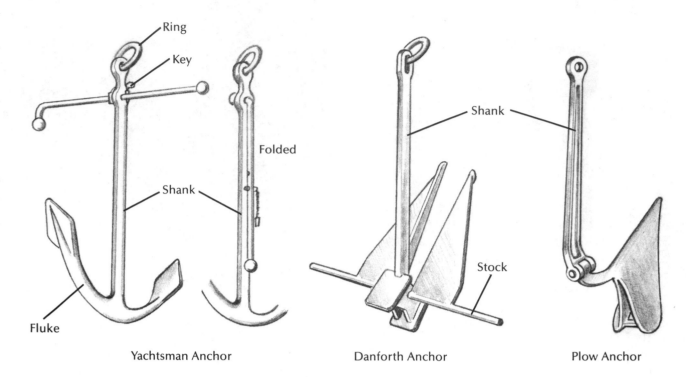

Ring

Key

Folded

Shank

Shank

Fluke

Shank

Stock

Yachtsman Anchor   Danforth Anchor   Plow Anchor

Figure 79. While the Yachtsman's anchor is the best one for rocky or weedy bottoms, the Danforth and the Plow are best in mud or sand, and are probably most suited to small boats. Cruising boats might carry two or more anchors.

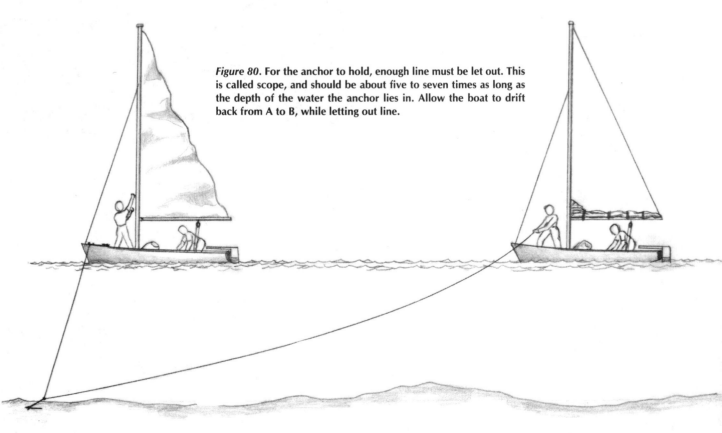

Figure 80. For the anchor to hold, enough line must be let out. This is called scope, and should be about five to seven times as long as the depth of the water the anchor lies in. Allow the boat to drift back from A to B, while letting out line.

A   B

Under most weather and sea conditions, regardless of water depth, an anchor holds best with a *scope* of seven to one. This means that seven lengths of anchor line are let out, each length corresponding to the depth of the water at the anchorage as measured from the bow chock. Shorter scope cannot be relied upon to hold when the wind blows, particularly when the scope is only three to one or less.

There are several ways to determine the depth of the water. One way is to measure with a *sounding lead;* another way is to put *fathom* markings (six feet equals one fathom) on your anchor line. This way the anchor line is also the sounding line. When you feel the anchor touch bottom, look for the nearest mark on the anchor line at a height equivalent to the bow chock. Then, knowing the depth, you can accurately measure out six more equal lengths of line. You then have enough for proper scope.

In some parts of the country, skippers carry poles, six- to eight-feet long. These poles usually have one-foot markings on them for measuring depth of water.

Before lowering the anchor, you must choose just the right spot for it, so that when you drift back on the line, you will end up in the place you've chosen for your boat—and at least three or four boat lengths from the nearest boat. Maneuver so that you can shoot up into the wind and have

the boat come to a stop right at the point where the anchor is to be lowered.

As your boat loses forward momentum, gently lower the hook until it touches the bottom; it is never thrown, or it is likely to snag on its own rode. Let the boat drift back two or three boat lengths while you pay out line, then snub the line gently around a cleat. As the boat drifts backward, maintain a light pressure to start the anchor digging in. Only then let the rest of the anchor line out and pay it out slowly as the boat drifts back. When the desired length of line is out, again snub the line around the anchor cleat; the firm tug will make doubly sure that the anchor has dug in well and is holding. Now make the line fast to the anchor cleat, with a hitch at the end.

Check your position relative to nearby boats and shore features, particularly those on either side. If your anchor drags, the angle between boats will change. If the angle remains the same, the anchor is holding.

Of course, should the boat drift because the anchor is not holding, you should immediately check for sufficient scope, then haul it up and try another spot.

Leaving the Anchorage

Leaving an anchorage is similar to leaving a mooring, once the anchor and its line are on

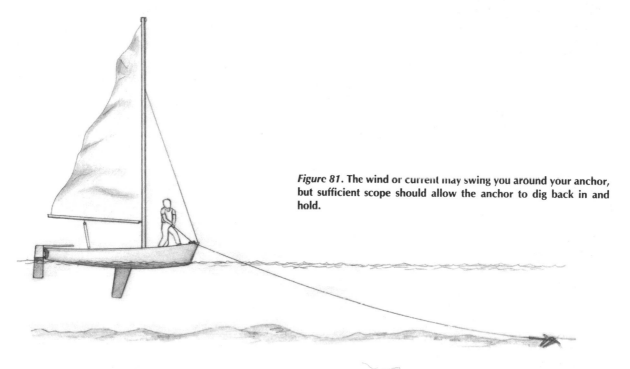

Figure 81. The wind or current may swing you around your anchor, but sufficient scope should allow the anchor to dig back in and hold.

Figure 82. When ready to leave, start by pulling up the rode and coiling it neatly on board. The mainsail should be raised or ready to raise before the anchor is broken out.

Figure 83. When the anchor comes up, it may be heavy with weed and mud. Dunk it a few times to clean it before bringing it aboard.

board. First, haul in the line until it is almost vertical and cleat it. Raise the mainsail, then uncleat the anchor line and haul up the anchor.

When the anchor comes above water, hold it there so it can be cleaned with a mop or sponge or by dunking it up and down in the water. When it is clean, bring it up on deck, coil the rode, and stow the anchor and rode below deck.

In a crowded anchorage it may be necessary to bend on and raise the jib before breaking out the anchor, so the boat can be brought under control as soon as the anchor is clear of the water. Care must be taken to keep the anchor and its line clear of the jib sheets so they won't be fouled or knock the anchor overboard as the jib is trimmed.

Where there is plenty of room for the boat to drift back, the jib is not bent on until the foredeck is clear. It is then raised, put aback, and the boat is put on course.

Anchoring Problems

Should the anchor be dropped where the bottom is known to be rocky, the anchor flukes may catch under a rock and be held fast, permanently. It is a wise precaution when anchoring in such a spot to tie a line to the crown of the anchor. With this line you will be able to lift and draw the anchor out, crown first if it is snagged.

This line can be attached to a float, with the line just long enough to reach the water's surface (allowing for the rise in tide), or the line can run to a foredeck cleat on the boat. In this case it must be longer than the anchor line itself, as this *trip line* should never come under any strain. An alternative is to use a shorter length of line and secure the end to the anchor line itself.

With a trip line attached, there must be someone aboard the boat *in constant attendance*.

Sometimes it is possible to break an anchor free by *sailing it out*. This is done by raising all sail, then sailing in a complete circle, maintaining full strain on the anchor by keeping the line taut. The pulling, turning effect might twist the anchor loose.

If you are a skin diver, there is nothing simpler than donning your fins and face mask and jumping overboard. Follow the rode down to the anchor and free it.

Figure 84. If a line has been led to the anchor's crown before setting it in rocky bottoms, it can be overturned and pulled free of the rocks.

Helpful Hints

SIX FACTORS THAT MUST BE TAKEN INTO ACCOUNT WHEN ANCHORING:

1—Protection of craft from wind and sea
2—Depth of water
3—Rise and fall of tide (if any)
4—Turning circle in relation to other boats should wind or tide change
5—Nature of bottom
6—Scope of anchor line

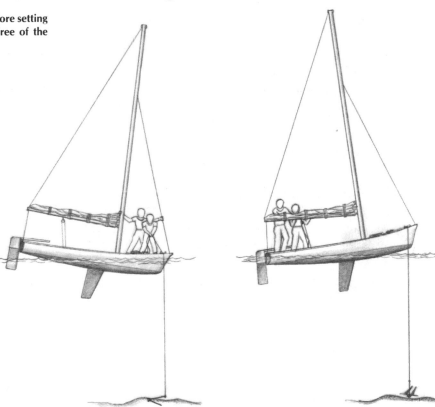

Figure 85. Using movable crew weight or a rising tide, the boat's buoyancy can break out a snagged anchor.

Should the anchor stick tightly in a muddy bottom, and it can't be raised by hand, have everyone on board move to the bow of the boat, haul in on the line until it is as straight and taut as possible, and make it fast to a cleat. Then have everyone move to the stern; the shift in weight will cause the bow to rise, breaking the anchor free. A rising tide can also help raise an anchor in this manner.

Permanent Moorings

Marine dealers often make up and sell a complete mooring system that meets local conditions and requirements. It is useful to know how such a system is made up and to know the points that should be checked periodically for excessive wear.

A mooring normally is comprised of several parts: the mushroom anchor, a cable which consists of heavy chain and light chain (or a combination of chain and line), the mooring pendant, and the mooring buoy or float. All these parts are held together in one continuous line by shackles or splices. Lengths and strengths of the components depend on the size and type of boat to be secured and the depth of the water. The larger the boat, the heavier the lines, chains, and anchor must be. When there is doubt about what sizes or weights are to be used, the heavier or larger size should be selected. A good, strong mooring assures the safety of the boat when the skipper is not on board.

Mooring floats should be painted in distinctive colors or markings, and the name of the boat lettered on; this is particularly important in a crowded anchorage where many floats may be the same shape or color. A fluorescent band on a float will reflect the beam of a flashlight at night.

Figure 86. Mooring equipment should be hauled and inspected every few years for wear and chafe.

Figure 87. Check each part of the mooring gear for wear, particularly at splices and at shackle points. The chain section should be one and one half times the maximum water depth.

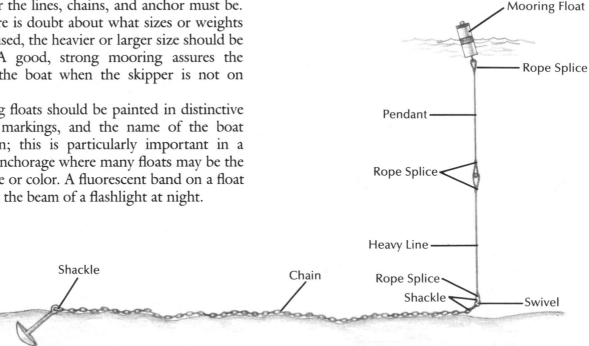

In general, the heavy line or light chain portion of the mooring system should be at least the maximum depth of the water; take into account any unusually high tides that may occur. The heavy chain is one and a half times this length. Depending on water depth, the pendant itself may be from half to full length of the maximum water depth. Note that in some systems, particularly where light chain is attached to the heavy chain, the pendant does not come between the light chain and the buoy, and the buoy remains in the water when the pendant is brought aboard the boat.

If there is unrestricted swinging room for the boat, combined lengths of chain and line (or heavy and light chain) should be five to seven times the depth of high water for safety in all but the most violent storms.

Note in Figure 87 the overhaul check points; these should be inspected at the start of the season and every six to eight weeks during the season.

Helpful Hints

USE OF SHOCK CORD
Shock cord, because of its strength and elasticity, is used to hold equipment in place. One end of the cord may be permanently fastened; the other end, with a loop in it, is stretched across the object and fastened to a hook. Paddles, lines, anchors, and other gear secured in this manner are released when needed by unhooking the cord. A length of shock cord with a loop in one end and a peg in the other end can be used to hold spinnaker booms and boathooks, to keep a topping lift taut, to keep halyards from slapping against the mast, or to serve as a sail stop.

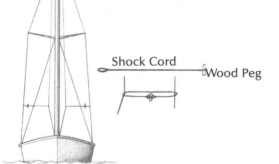

Shock Cord — Wood Peg

COCKPIT COVER
A cockpit cover is essential for keeping rain out of the boat when she lies unattended at her mooring. An ideal type of cover for a small boat is shown on the right. It is closed in front but open at the after end to allow venti-

lation. It hangs over the boom and is fastened in front by a collar around the mast. Lines hold the lower forward ends to the shrouds. The after end is held by a line tied to the boom. Snaps just under the rail hold the sides in place and prevent them from blowing out.

Open End

SOUNDING LINE
A strong fishing line, tied to a three-pound sinker, makes a good *sounding (lead)* line for a small boat. It is compact and easily stowed. Mark the line in the following manner: Measure off six feet (one fathom) from the sinker and tie in a marker; measure out additional six-foot lengths and add additional markers until you have a line long enough for your needs.

By hollowing out the bottom end of the sinker enough to hold a bit of wax, it is possible to "arm" the lead. When the line is lowered and the weight touches the bottom, portions of the bottom will adhere to the wax, indicating whether it is mud, sand, or gravel.

5

Safe Sailing

Handled properly, small sailboats are quite safe in all normal conditions of wind and sea. A prudent skipper does not go out when winds are obviously too strong or bad weather is forecast, but there are times when a sudden and unusually strong wind, a *squall,* comes up, and you are caught out on the water. How you handle yourself and your boat is of utmost importance if you are to avoid accident to sail, rigging, and possibly yourself.

Too Much Wind

In storm conditions you must be constantly alert to wind and wave and the reactions of the boat. Keep an eye out for boats around you, for they may get the wind first; how these boats are handled will be a clue to what to expect and what you will have to do when the wind strikes.

The first thing to do when a sudden puff of wind strikes is to *luff up:* steer your boat closer to the eye of the wind. Ease sheets as much as needed. By easing the sheets as you head closer to the wind, you spill the wind in the sails; otherwise wind pressure may capsize your boat before you can hike out for balance.

If the strong wind increases, drop the sails. The main may be lowered first because it usually has the greater sail area. As the sail comes down, gather it in, lean on it, and hold it down until it is tied up and furled securely. If you let sails lie loose, the wind will get into them, raise them, and could slam the boat over.

In case of a line squall, the long, low, rapidly advancing black cloud that can be spotted before the wind strikes, round up and drop sail immediately; then run under bare poles, without any sail up, before the wind. If your boat begins to travel too fast, you can slow down by trailing a bucket over the stern or even the anchor line.

If you are ever in doubt about the force of the wind or whether to carry sail or not, drop the sails for safety.

If you are close to a lee shore or a hazard that could damage the boat—or the storm is pushing you out to sea—drop your anchor. Let out as much anchor line as possible; the greater the

Helpful Hint

HAUL THE BOAT IN EXTREME WEATHER
In bad storms, small-boat skippers should check mooring gear to insure the safety of the boat. When warned by the National Weather Service of the approach of an extremely strong blow, boats in an exposed anchorage should be hauled out, if possible, and protected from wind and waves. Though a boat may have oversize mooring equipment, the surge of the sea can often upset centerboard boats. Also, other vessels that have broken loose from their moorings can drift down and damage your boat.

Figure 88. While these sailors look happy, they ought to give some thought to reducing sail soon, perhaps by dousing the mainsail, as the boat beyond them has prudently done. They already have a full luff in the mainsail and considerable weight on the windward rail. With just a little more wind, something has got to go.

scope, the better the likelihood the anchor will hold. If you have a spare line aboard of adequate strength, you can add it to your anchor line by tying a bowline (see Chapter 7) in one line through a bowline in the other. Cleat the anchor line first at a point ahead of the bitter end; secure the bitter end of the second line. Then uncleat the anchor line and pay out the balance of both lines. The line must always be firmly secured to the boat.

When wind strength permits some sail to be carried safely, there are a number of ways it can be done, depending on boat type and wind strength.

Where the wind is excessive only in puffs, it may be possible to carry both main and jib trimmed tight and the mainsail luffing. This takes the boat through the puffs and keeps good speed on the boat. Some of the pressure on the main is relieved, thereby keeping the boat more upright. Let the jib backwind the main; if the jib is allowed to flap wildly, it might tear. The main should luff but still have drive in the aft end of the sail.

Be ready to release both jib and main sheets quickly should the wind force become too great.

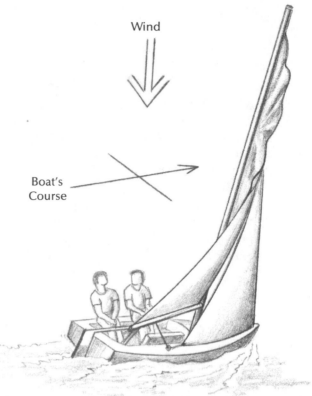

Figure 89. In a puff, it may be possible to spill wind from the mainsail and continue sailing on a reach. If in doubt about the strength of a puff, douse a sail.

Figure 90. With jibs and mainsails luffing, these racers have all the wind they can handle without reducing sail.

Hold both sheets by hand if possible or with a turn under a cleat if there's too much of a strain. Sit up on the high side and help balance the boat by leaning to windward.

If you have to sail in a strong wind, a reach is the safest point of sailing. Constant adjustment of the sails against the wind will keep the boat in as upright a position as possible. East sheets and luff up in the puffs, bear off and haul in sheets when the wind lets up. Always try to keep the boat moving, to increase both stability and maneuverability. Have just enough sail to provide driving power—both main and jib will luff partly in this situation, with only the aft edges of both sails furnishing drive to the boat.

Sailing with jib alone is the easiest and safest method to follow when wind is too strong for both sails to be up. You are then under as short canvas as possible (except for a storm jib).

Figure 92. **With a reefed main and doused jib, these sailors are doing fine in rough conditions.**

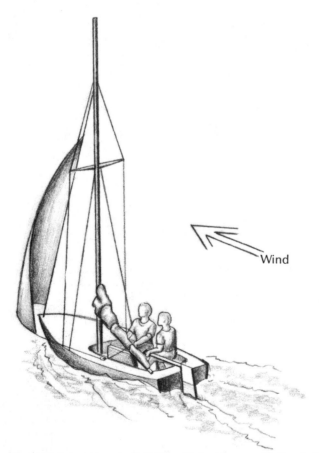

Figure 91. **In a severe squall, it is usually best to run with the wind with the smallest possible sail up, usually the jib.**

It is surprising how well you can reach and often how high you can point with jib alone. You have control of the course to sail, to a degree, though your leeway will be greater than usual. Running before the wind or reaching is much steadier and easier than trying to beat to windward. Sit on the high side of the boat or in the bottom of the cockpit to help keep the boat upright. Do not cleat the jib; hold it in your hands, easing the strain by leading it under a cleat.

In some cases it is best to sail under just the main. You have better control on a reach than when sailing with the jib alone, but more sail area is exposed to the wind. The boat will heel more with the varying force of the wind—but you will have greater speed through the water.

You can luff more easily in strong wind puffs and more quickly, too, and a weather helm condition is created that automatically will bring the boat up into the wind should you let go of the tiller.

Figure 93. **These sailors on the rail should keep an eye on that dark cloud ahead, and on the other boats around them.**

Keep the crew on the windward side and lean outward during the puffs to help keep the boat as upright as possible.

Coming About Instead of Jibing

When you are running in strong winds and rough seas and you need to tack, do not try to jibe across the wind. Instead, head up into the wind and come about. In these conditions, the action of the sea and the height of the waves play an important part in this maneuver.

Generally there are three or four high, steep waves, then a series of short rollers, then three or four more steep ones, and so on. The trick is to come about when the seas run low. Good helmsmanship, good judgment, and good timing all play their parts.

Do not come around fast. Make a big, wide loop; broad reach first, then swing to a close reach.

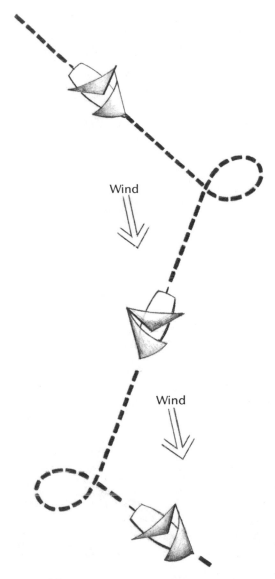

Figure 94. **While it may seem like a roundabout course, it is a safe practice to come about and make a near-full circle instead of jibing in high seas and lots of wind.**

Time yourself so that when the seas run low, you can come about quickly. When the sails are on the opposite side, let the sheets out (see that they don't snarl) as you fall off onto a reach. As soon as everything is settled, you can ease the sheet more and run again before the wind on the new tack.

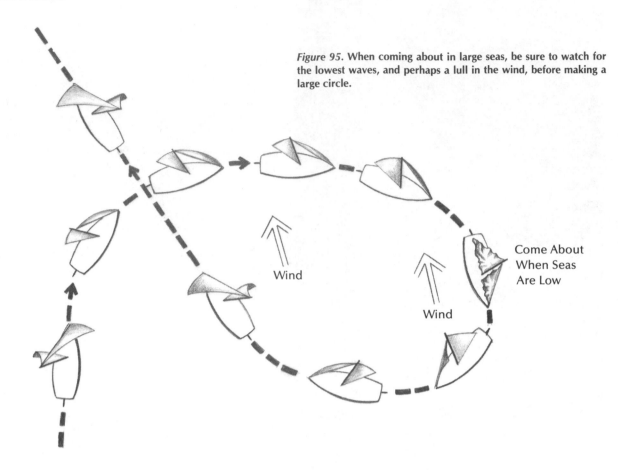

Figure 95. When coming about in large seas, be sure to watch for the lowest waves, and perhaps a lull in the wind, before making a large circle.

Wind

Wind

Come About
When Seas
Are Low

Precautions to Take Before a Squall Strikes

1—Head the boat into the wind.
2—Ease all the sheets.
3—Lower the centerboard all the way.
4—Lower one or both sails; furl and stop them.
5—Secure all loose gear, including floorboards, that might float away.
6—Put on Life Jackets.
7—Watch the weather.
8—Watch other boats nearby.

Figure 96. Sailing into the dark clouds ahead, this crew has wisely prepared themselves with foul-weather gear and they are ready to leap forward to shorten sail as soon as it's necessary.

If You Capsize

A boat may capsize when least expected. Sometimes a capsize is unavoidable, but more often it is due to a lack of caution, inexperienced boat handling, or a misjudgment of wind force. The sudden shift of wind in a squall, too much wind for the amount of sail being carried, jibing in a strong wind (particularly if the centerboard is up), and improper weight distribution in the hull all may lead to a capsize.

Since most capsizes are associated with squall winds, the safety measures noted earlier in this chapter will prevent them from happening. These precautions are shown in the box on page 70, along with additional steps that the prudent skipper can take for the safety of his boat and crew.

In strong winds when any sail is carried, placement of crew and other weights is important. If too much weight is to leeward, for example, the chance of a capsize is greater than with weight to windward. Obviously, the boat's center of gravity is on the wrong side. Not so obvious is what can happen if weight is too far forward and the boat is running before the wind. Here the boat may literally dive into a wave and not be able to rise to free herself. The momentum and the force of the wind will swing her broadside, where the wind can knock her down.

Do not take chances; if there is any doubt about what the weather is going to do, take all necessary precautions. This is the mark of an experienced skipper.

In spite of every precaution, capsizes can occur, and you must know what to do when your boat goes over. The first rule is to stick with the boat, which should have enough built-in or added flotation material to stay afloat. After getting over the first surprise of finding yourself in the water, swim to the boat and stay with her.

Make sure that all the crew are accounted for and able to take care of themselves. Occasionally someone may get hit on the head with the boom, get caught under a sail, or become entangled with

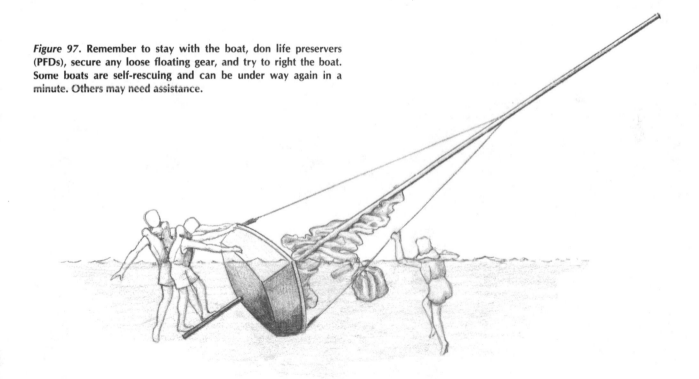

Figure 97. Remember to stay with the boat, don life preservers (PFDs), secure any loose floating gear, and try to right the boat. Some boats are self-rescuing and can be under way again in a minute. Others may need assistance.

the lines, and may need assistance. Get to the life preservers and put them on if they're not already on. Take off shoes and excess clothing. It should be possible to make a bundle of these items that can be lashed to the boat with the end of a sheet or any other loose line available. If any boat gear was not properly secured, it will be floating around you; try to lash the gear together and then fasten the bundle to a cleat or to the mast.

Many modern boats are designed to be self-rescuing and can be easily righted and sailed on without lowering sails or even bailing the cockpit. You should stand on the centerboard of a capsized self-rescuing boat and raise the boat so her bow will be into the wind and sails free to luff. Then climb aboard, gather any gear that may be adrift, and continue sailing, with a little more caution. The forward motion of the boat should drain the cockpit of water after sailing a short distance.

Some older boats, however, are more difficult to right, and the worse-case procedure is described below. You'll have to experiment to find the best and safest method of righting your boat.

Before attempting to right the boat, you may have to take off the sails. Begin with the mainsail. Release the main halyard, but make the end fast so it won't get away and entangle the swimmers; pull the sail down the mast—a slow, difficult job with the sail flat in the water. Pull it all the way to the boom and furl it as best as you can. It can be secured with an extra piece of line or the main sheet.

Now do the same with the jib, and then make all sheets and halyards fast. You don't want them floating around where they will get in your way. Work slowly; take a breather now and then if necessary. Do not tire yourself.

If the centerboard is up, release its pendant so it can be lowered. The board should be pulled out as far as possible. Swim around to the bottom of the boat; now stand on the bottom end of the centerboard and take a grip on the shrouds, a cleat, or the rail. Lean backward and push down on the board while hauling on the boat.

The boat should right herself slowly. She may be unwieldy and difficult to control in her swamped condition, but in most cases she will be able to support the weight of the crew, who must climb in over the stern. The sometimes long process of bailing should begin, using a bucket if available, or bailer, until the boat is stable enough to raise sail and continue on.

Narrow cockpits and wide side decks, such as those on Star class racing sloops, minimize the danger of swamping when a boat takes a hard knockdown, but almost any boat, particularly those with centerboards, will flip over once the angle of heel exceeds a certain point. Keelboats,

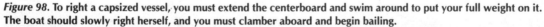

Figure 98. To right a capsized vessel, you must extend the centerboard and swim around to put your full weight on it. The boat should slowly right herself, and you must clamber aboard and begin bailing.

with their heavy outside ballast, are more difficult to capsize: the further they heel, the greater the righting force that is developed; also, as with any boat, the greater the angle of heel, the less pressure there is on the sails. This combination reduces the likelihood of a keelboat capsizing.

Tips for Rescue and Escort Boats

Approach and maneuver from the lee side of a capsized boat. With the engine in neutral, the rescue vessel will not drift down on the distressed boat. Be sure to keep clear of all lines that might snag the propeller.

Pass a towline to the crew of the capsized boat, have it led through the bow chocks and then made fast to the mast. If the line is made fast to a cleat, the cleat may pull out when a heavy strain is taken on the towline. Get the crew from the distressed boat aboard by throwing each swimmer a line and hauling them to the rescue vessel one by one. If the rescue boat has high topsides, rig a ladder over the side to make it easier for the wet crew to climb aboard. If they have been in cold water, rub them down with towels and cover them with blankets until the shivering stops. Hot drinks—but no alcoholic stimulants—can be given.

If the distressed boat is upright and ready to be towed, put the strongest of the crew back on board (or one of your crew, if he or she can be spared for the job) to steer. If the centerboard can be raised, the rudder unshipped, and all water pumped out, all of the rescued can stay aboard the rescue vessel because their boat will tow easily without the aid of a helmsman.

Try to pick up all loose floating gear belonging to a boat that has capsized.

Take up strain on the towline slowly and proceed slowly. The towed boat, full of water, will be very sluggish and will be under strains that the hull was not meant to withstand. Water weighs from 62.2 to 64 pounds per cubic foot; in the swamped hull of a small sailboat, this can come close to two tons. The rescue vessel will be towing all this extra weight.

Figure 99. If towing is necessary, it should be done slowly and carefully. A crew member should be put in the boat to steer.

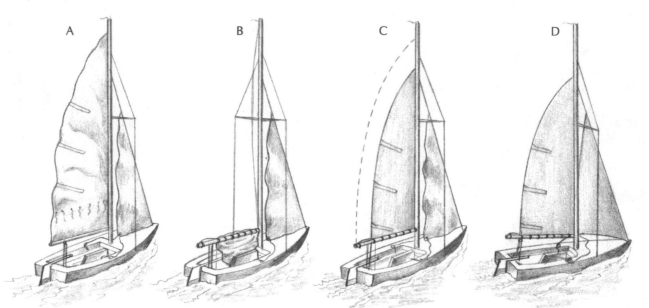

Figure 100. To reef in the traditional manner, the mainsail is lowered completely to tie in the reef points at B. The rehoisted sail at C shows how much sail area has been reduced. Under way again at D, the boat should heel less and be just as fast.

Reefing

Reefing is a means of reducing sail area so that a boat can continue to sail safely in stronger than normal winds. Many small boats are not equipped for reefing on the theory that they are never so far from shelter that they can't be brought out of harm's way before a storm strikes; others, used for racing, are not so equipped because the skippers feel the *reef points* (see Figure 101) detract from the efficiency of the mainsail. However, some small boats and almost all larger ones have some means of reducing sail area, and the process of reefing should be understood.

There are three methods commonly used for reefing: traditional reefing, roller reefing, and slab or jiffy reefing. In traditional reefing, a line of reef points, parallel to the boom, holds down a section of sail and ties that section up securely. In roller reefing, the foot of the sail is rolled around the boom, which has special reefing gears at the gooseneck. Jiffy reefing is a variation of the traditional method in which reef points are not used. In any case, reefing must be done properly to avoid tearing the sail or pulling it out of shape.

For traditional reefing, the boat is steered upwind, and the jib is kept full to steady the boat. Keeping speed up on the boat will increase stability in a rough and rolling sea. The boom crotch is

put in place, and the boom is dropped into it as the mainsail is lowered. Lower the main all the way, gathering it in as it comes down so that it doesn't fly into the water. Haul the mainsheet in tight and make it fast; this keeps the boom from jumping out of the crotch. Some skippers leave the mainsail partly hoisted, but it may pull and flap in the strong wind, hindering the operation, or a gust may fill the sail and capsize the boat.

Have two short pieces of line handy, each about five or six feet in length. Take one of the pieces and lash the *tack ring* (see Figure 101) to the boom. Now take the leech ring; pull straight along the boom and away from the mast. Keep the canvas straight and even. With the other piece of line, lash this ring to the boom, pass the ends of the line through the ring again, and bring them aft to the outhaul or boom end to secure them.

Take the part of the sail that is between the reef and the boom and pull this through to one side. Pull this flap out as evenly as possible, roll it up neatly, and tuck the roll between the reef points and the boltrope at the foot of the sail, leaving the reef points free. Tie this roll together with the reef points, using a reef (square) knot or slippery reef knot (see Chapter 7). The reef points go under the boltrope, not around the boom; make sure the

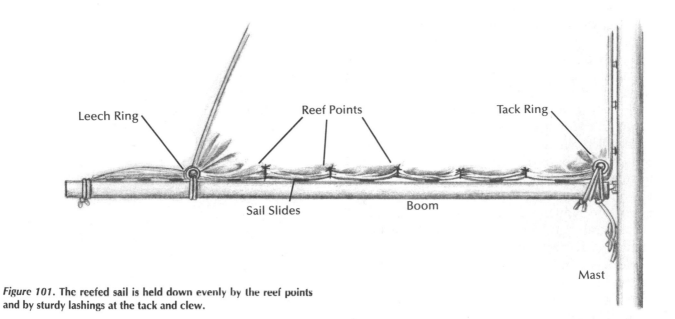

Figure 101. The reefed sail is held down evenly by the reef points and by sturdy lashings at the tack and clew.

Labels in figure: Leech Ring, Reef Points, Tack Ring, Sail Slides, Boom, Mast

knots are tight and in an even line.

To raise the sail, ease the main sheet; haul on the main halyard, and as soon as the boom clears the crotch, remove the crotch and stow it out of the way so it will not foul the boom as the main fills. Check all the lashings and knots for an even strain and be sure that all are securely tied. Trim the jib and get under way.

Figure 103. A properly reefed mainsail should be smooth along the foot and should set just as well as a full main.

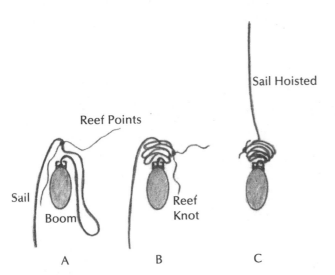

Figure 102. At A, the reef points are threaded between the boom and the slides of the lowered sail, and secured around the loose flap of sail, as at B. The sail is hoisted again at C.

Labels in figure: Reef Points, Sail Hoisted, Sail, Boom, Reef Knot, A, B, C

There can be a disadvantage in keeping the jib up with a crew of only two, for one has to steer and control the boat. The other person has to do all of the reefing and moving about, making it necessary to work with just one hand, as the other is needed to hold on. If necessary, drop the jib during the reefing process.

In roller reefing, the mainsail is not dropped all the way. The boom fitting is cranked with a special handle to wrap the sail around the boom as the halyard is eased; the mainsheet is slacked just enough to reduce tension on the sail so it will roll evenly and tightly onto the boom. Usually the crank and halyard can be handled by one person while a second crew member steers; thus this method is suitable for a shorthanded crew.

When sail area has been reduced to the desired size, the main halyard is cleated, and the mainsheet is trimmed as necessary. Note that as the sail is brought down, slides near its foot must be slipped out of the mast track to permit the sail to roll onto the boom. It may also be necessary to remove the lowest batten.

In jiffy reefing, only the tack and clew are lashed to the boom. The tack ring is pulled down to the boom as the sail is lowered by a line that runs from the boom up through the ring and back down to the boom. Note that the sail is not lowered all the way; as soon as the tack ring is down to the boom, the halyard is secured, and the tack ring is also secured to the boom. This will leave the outer end of the boom sagging low. It is pulled up to the leech ring by a line which runs from a point on the boom abaft the ring, up through the ring, back down to the boom. This line is then led forward to a cleat on the boom. See Figure 102.

The pocket formed by the reef may be allowed to flap, or the sail may have reef points that can be used in the traditional manner.

The advantage of slab or jiffy reefing is that it is very quick. The mainsail is not dropped, and the jib can remain up if there is enough crew that the tiller can remain manned.

Undoing (*shaking out*) a reef is done by reversing the steps in the order in which the reef was originally tied. For traditional reefing, for example, this means luffing into the wind, lowering the mainsail into its crotch while hauling the sheet tight, untying the reef points, then the leech and tack rings in that order. The sail is then raised so that wrinkles formed in the sail by the reef can come out.

Storm Sails

Storm sails are small but very strong sails that can be set when the wind is too strong for reefed sails. Storm sails are not normally found on boats used for instruction, for day sailing, or for day racing.

Helpful Hint

SAIL REPAIR
Keep on hand a roll of wide stick-on sail-repair tape, available from marine dealers. It is most useful in making a quick repair to a torn sail. The illustration shows how a long, wide piece follows the length of the tear and is reinforced, in turn, by shorter, narrower crosspieces. This prevents further tearing of the sail until it can be permanently repaired by a sailmaker.

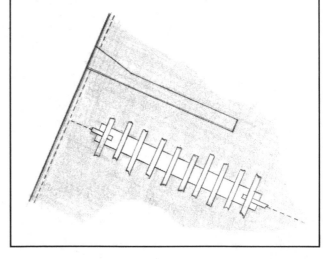

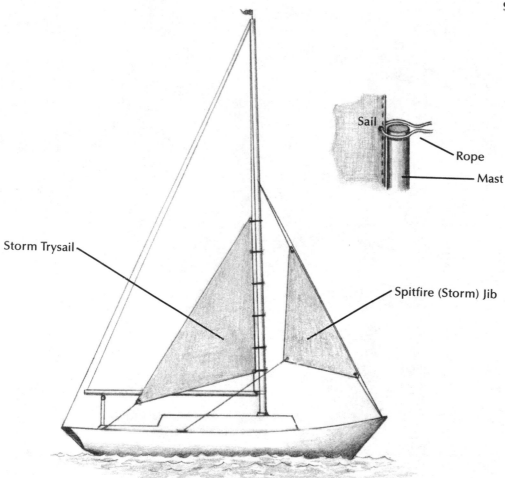

Figure 104. Storm sails are made of very heavy material to withstand high winds. Be sure to know how they fit on your boat before they are really needed.

They should be carried aboard boats used for extended cruising, particularly if long, offshore passages are involved. The two storm sails are the *spitfire* or *storm jib* and the *storm trysail*.

The storm jib is a small-size working jib made from heavy material to withstand heavy winds. Its purpose is to balance sail area so the boat will steer more easily with a reefed mainsail or storm trysail. It is made exactly like a jib and handles the same way. The storm jib is hoisted high off the deck to prevent waves from washing into it.

The storm trysail is a triangular loose-footed sail made from heavy material. It is larger than a storm jib and is set in place of a mainsail. Instead of sail slides, it may carry lines sewn into the luff at intervals to tie around the mast.

A large trysail may be set in lieu of a reefed mainsail if the boat is to be kept on course; such a sail would carry slides for the mast track. Its clew would be hauled taut to the end of the boom, and sail trim is controlled in the normal manner by the mainsheet. A smaller trysail may be used when the boat must *heave to*—maintain her position in regard to the wind while slowly drifting leeward. For this use, the clew is hauled tight on the leeward side to a deck fitting. It is not attached to the boom, which should be lashed down in its crotch.

6

Beyond Basics

Once the procedures are learned for handling a boat under jib and mainsail, you can move on to the use of sails such as *genoas* and *spinnakers*. While these sails are seldom found on the small day sailers generally used by beginners, they are almost always found on larger boats used for cruising, racing, or both. The genoa is a triangular headsail much larger than the working job. It is used in place of the jib to provide more drive when reaching or beating. The spinnaker is also a large headsail; it replaces the jib when the boat is running before the wind or on a broad reach.

The Genoa

The genoa, also known as a *genoa jib,* overlaps the mainsail, which means it must be set outside the shrouds and the sheets led well aft. A sheet winch must be used because of the extra forces exerted by the sail, and there must be enough crew to handle the sheets even with the winches.

When coming about, the clew of this sail must work itself forward, past the shrouds, and drag itself around the mast. The sheet must be released in ample time for this to happen. Therefore the boat is brought about more slowly than with a working jib, and care and judgment must be exercised to prevent the boat from going into irons. The longer sheets needed to control this sail drag against the rigging and prevent the sail from swinging over easily. Often a crew member has to take the clew, run forward with it, and lead it around the shrouds and mast to the other side. Sometimes the sheet or the sail itself will snag on a

Figure 105. This roller furling genoa is easy to handle, even though it is a large sail. The colored edges are a layer of material sewn onto the sail to protect it from the ultraviolet rays of the sun when the sail is rolled up.

projection, such as a cleat or winch on the mast, as it flaps its way from one side of the boat to the other.

Two or more genoas of varying size may be carried in a boat's sail locker, with the largest made of the lightest material, for the lightest winds, and the smallest sail of the heaviest material, for stronger winds. In some rigs, where the mainsail is relatively small, the genoa may provide the greater driving force.

Because the genoa adds a lot more sail area, the boat must be designed for the sail, or she will be thrown out of balance. Undesirable lee helm is developed, making it necessary to work the tiller constantly to keep the boat on course.

The Spinnaker

In general, today's spinnaker is a half-egg-shaped nylon sail that billows out at the top and curves in at the sides so that it receives lift as well as forward drive from the wind. Some spinnakers are bulbous, some spherical, some long and relatively narrow, depending on the design, and the ideas of the skippers and their sailmakers.

Figure 106. **The spinnaker is a light nylon sail that is set on a downwind course. The sail requires a spinnaker pole and its own halyard and sheets.**

The sail is used effectively when sailing before the wind and when reaching. In light air it does more to keep the boat moving than the mainsail; in a strong wind it exerts tremendous pull and can be quite difficult to handle.

Spinnakers are made of the lightest nylon so they can readily lift and fill out in the most feathery airs. The parts of the sail, as shown in Figure 107, are the head at the top corner, the foot at the bottom edge, the leeches at both sides, and the clews at both lower corners. There is no tack and no luff, except when the sail is set.

One corner or clew of this sail, when in use, is held out on a pole called a *spinnaker pole*. The inboard end of the pole is attached to the mast, and the pole is held up not by the sail but by a pole lift, and it can be moved forward and aft or up and down. Its forward or aft movement is controlled

Figure 107. **The spinnaker pole should always be controlled by its pole lift to hold it up, and its foreguy to hold it down. The guy controls the pole and the spinnaker together, while the sheet controls only the spinnaker.**

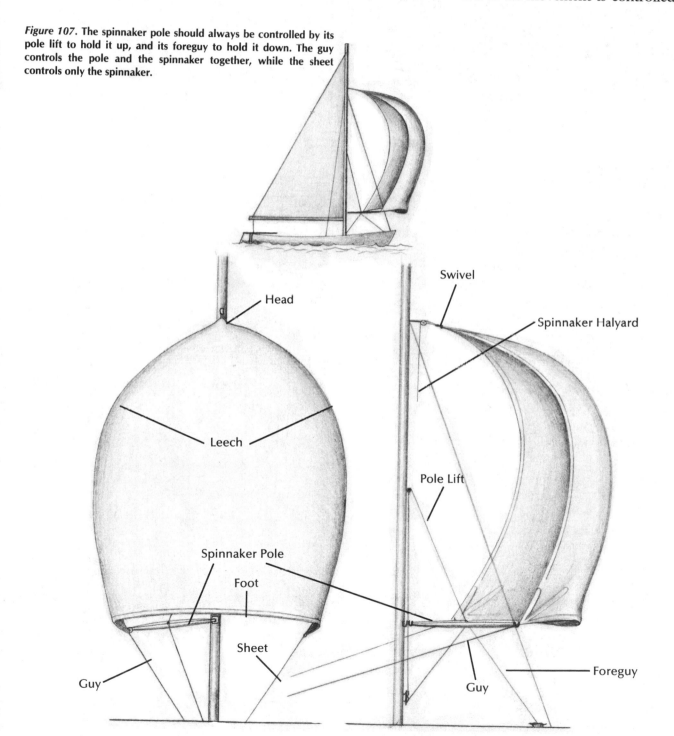

Figure 108. In a race, colorful spinnakers sprout from every boat, while the jibs have been lowered to give the spinnakers more clear air.

by two lines called *guys*. The other corner or clew of the sail is held out and up by the wind but is controlled by an attached line, the *spinnaker sheet*.

The after guy and sheet are interchangeable, depending on which side of the boat the spinnaker pole is set. They usually are the same type of line; only the name is changed to suit their use at any given time. The guy always leads from the clew attached to the spinnaker pole, and the sheet always leads from the loose-flying clew.

The up and down movement of the spinnaker pole is controlled by a foreguy, a line led from the outer end of the pole to the foredeck. In some cases a *pole downhaul* is used for this; it is rigged to the middle of the spar, along with a *pole lift*, and both are adjustable, along with the foreguy.

When a boat is running before the wind and jibes onto the opposite tack, the spinnaker pole is released from one clew and reattached to the opposite clew. There are several ways to accomplish this; all are beyond the scope of this book, and the process involves a high degree of skill and teamwork on the part of the crew, particularly when racing.

Other Types of Rig

While the small sloop, with a single mast, mainsail, and jib, is the most popular rig for learning to

Figure 109. A sloop may be of any size, but always has one mast, with a mainsail and only one headsail at a time.

Figure 110. A catboat has only one sail, usually a gaff-rigged mainsail of considerable size.

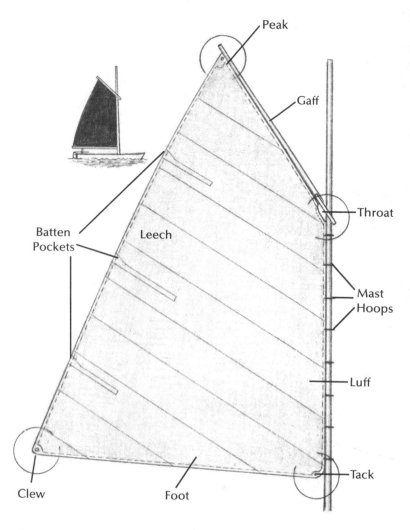

Figure 111. The gaff-rigged mainsail is an older rig that is still seen frequently on the water. The four-sided sail is held at its upper edge by a spar called a gaff, and at its luff by wooden mast hoops.

sail, there are a number of other popular rigs on cruising and racing sailboats.

A sloop, for example, may have a high-aspect ratio or low-aspect ratio rig. The "aspect" depends on the relative height of the mast and length of the boom in relation to hull size. In general, a modern high-aspect ratio rig is most efficient, as most of the driving force of a sail is developed along its leading edge.

The mainsail on most modern boats is of the jib-headed or Marconi type, as noted in Chapter 1. Some older boats and some new "character boat" types may carry a *gaff rig*. This is a four-sided sail as shown in Figure 111. A *gaff* carries the upper edge of the sail.

Mast hoops hold the sail to the mast. The gaff sail was the rule, rather than the exception, until naval architects realized the analogy between wind action on a sail and the lift provided by an airplane wing. Gaff sails are not nearly as efficient as the jib-headed type.

Sailboards, like the Sunfish, which are somewhat like large surfboards with a mast and sail, usually carry a single *lateen sail,* which has a spar along its leading edge as well as along the foot. The two spars are secured to the mast, with a portion of the sail projecting ahead of the mast; see Figure 112.

A more recent boat is the *board sailer,* on which the single crew member stands and steers by shifting his or her weight or the rig. These boats

feature a *wishbone rig*. This is a loose-footed sail with a curved double-boom arrangement as shown in Figure 113.

On larger hulls, rigs may be *cutter, yawl, ketch,* or *schooner*. A cutter, like a sloop, carries a single mast, but it is stepped further aft than a sloop's mast, and two headsails are carried: a *staysail* just ahead of the mast and the jib ahead of this; (Figure 114).

Yawls and *ketches* both have two masts, with the taller mast forward. There is no clear-cut distinction between the two types, but the yawl generally has a very small aftermast, the *mizzen*, stepped behind the rudderpost. The *mizzen* is necessarily quite small, although it can be extremely effective in helping to balance the boat. The mizzen mast on a ketch is stepped ahead of the rudderpost, and the sail is somewhat larger. It can contribute more to the driving power of the boat; the mainsail will be smaller than a sloop's mainsail. The combination of smaller main and mizzen make sail handling easier for a shorthanded crew.

Figure 112. Sailboards, like these Sunfish, are popular for beginners and experts alike.

Figure 113. New on the scene is the boardsailer, with a surfboard-type hull and a movable sail. It has no sheets, no rudder, and no shrouds, but steers by fore-and-aft balance of the rig.

Figure 114. A cutter has one mast, usually stepped quite far aft, and carries two headsails at once. Compared to a sloop with the same total sail area, the cutter's sails will all be smaller and easier to handle.

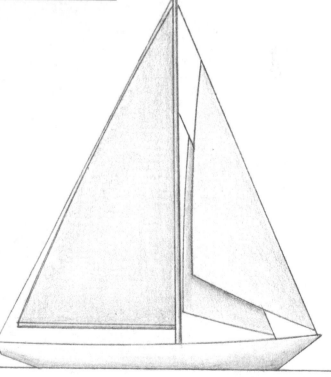

Figure 115. A yawl has a small mizzen that is used mostly to balance the sail plan and ease the work of the helmsman.

A *schooner* may have two or more masts; they may all be of the same height, but usually the tallest mast will be the aftermast. Very few schooners carry more than two masts. The tall aftermast is the mainmast and carries the mainsail; the forward mast is the *foremast,* and the sail it carries on its after side is the *foresail.* One or more headsails may be set ahead of the foremast (see Figure 121), and several different sails can be set between the masts.

Tuning Up

Correct adjustment of the standing rigging is an important aspect of getting safe, fast performance from a boat, and the correct rigging and tuning of sailing craft have puzzled sailors since they first went to sea.

The mast must be straight athwartships at all times: it must not favor one side over the other, or there will be a decided difference in the boat's ability to go to windward on one tack or the other. The mast step should be checked to see that the

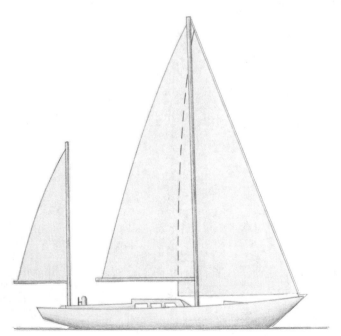

Figure 116. The yawl's mizzen mast is stepped aft of the helm, and the mizzen is very small.

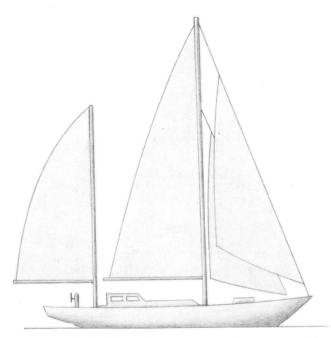

Figure 117. The ketch has a larger mizzen, and the mizzen mast is stepped farther forward, usually forward of the helm.

Figure 118. Compared to the yawl on the page opposite, this ketch has a large mizzen that can provide considerable drive by itself.

Figure 119. Many schooners have a combination of triangular mainsail and gaff foresail. This one has only one large headsail, making the boat easier to tack.

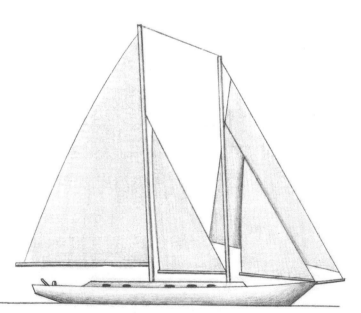

Figure 120. A staysail schooner has all-triangular sails and may be easier to handle than a gaff-rigged schooner.

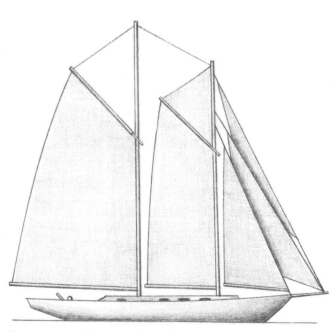

Figure 121. A gaff-rigged schooner has a four-sided mainsail on the taller aftermost mast.

heel of the mast is centered and that it cannot move. One way to make certain that the mast is correctly positioned and that the masthead is directly over the boat's centerline is to measure the masthead's distance from each side of the boat. This can be done by running a steel tape measure up to the masthead attached to the main halyard and measuring the distance from a common point. If a steel tape measure is not handy, the halyard itself can be used, but be careful to stretch it evenly.

The lower shrouds should be slacker than the uppers. This will compensate for the stretch of the longer upper shrouds. If the lowers are set up as tight as the uppers, stretch in the uppers will allow the masthead to fall off the centerline.

Rake of the mast determines in part what sort of helm the boat will carry when working to windward. Presumably the architect has considered the factors which make *your* boat go to weather and has raked the mast accordingly. After sailing a few times in average conditions, you may find this balance doesn't satisfy your requirements.

The average boat should have little or no helm in light going. When the wind pipes up, there should be some weather helm, but the boat's tendency to head into the wind should not be excessive. If there is too much weather helm, decrease the amount of rake until the helm becomes docile. You may find that your boat will sail fastest and most comfortably with the mast plumb or even raked far forward. There are other factors which may affect the helm, such as an improperly shaped mainsail.

If your boat has a lee helm, rake the mast further aft; by doing so that uncomfortable feeling of fighting to keep your boat up on course should disappear.

In the initial phase, however, with the rake adjusted to match the sail plan, the head stay and backstay are adjusted. (If your mast has *jumper stays*, they should be set up fairly taut before the mast is stepped, tight enough so that the top of the mast bends forward slightly until the backstay is taken up. While the shrouds can be slightly slack, the stays generally should be taut at all times except when running before the wind. If the head stay is slack, the jib will sag off, and its efficiency

Figure 122. A well-tuned rig makes sailing seem effortless and simple.

will be tremendously impaired. If the backstay is too loose, the weight of the jib will tend to make the mast bend forward, and the set of the mainsail will be seriously impaired. When the boat is not in use, it is often a good idea to release tension by slacking off a few turns on the backstay turnbuckle.

Comparatively recently, innovators have found that if the head of the mast is made to bend aft by tightening the backstay, the sail flattens and becomes more efficient when going to windward in a hard breeze. Putting a bend in the mast also tends to tighten the head stay, rendering the jib more efficient.

Most large boats and many small ones are now equipped with easily adjustable backstay turnbuckles for this reason. Slacking the head stay in small boats without backstays often has the same effect in a breeze. The head of the mast will bow aft, and the draft in the sail will disappear. However, be sure your mast does not need the full support of the head stay to keep from breaking.

Another reason for using adjustable backstay

turnbuckles is that they permit the release of tension when reaching and running before the wind. A boat seems to go much better reaching or running if the mast is not strapped down rigidly. Whether this is because there is more draft in the sail or because the whole rig is less rigid and is able to spring is uncertain; whatever the cause, it seems to work.

Once the initial adjustments to shrouds and stays are made, go for a sail and try for perfection. Pick a day when winds are most like those you will encounter during the season. Use the sails that you expect will provide the most efficiency in this wind. Do not make the mistake of going out shorthanded and using your working jib if you are going to spend the summer racing under a large genoa. Have enough crew to trim your sails efficiently, and have a competent helmsman at the tiller or wheel. The latter is important because the skipper should spend his time alternately sighting up the mast and adjusting the shrouds and stays.

Before making adjustments to shrouds after sailing on one tack, try the other tack to see if any problems that were evident on the one tack also show up on the other tack. Then make any necessary adjustments and make them gradually—a turn

or two at a time. Sight up the mast after each adjustment and work on only one adjustment at a time so that you can tell what effect the change had. Remember that adjusting includes loosening as well as tightening.

After you get the rig the way you want it, bend over the cotter pins or secure safety wire to each turnbuckle. Then place tape around these sharp points to protect the sail.

Unfortunately, after all these measures have been taken, tuning is not concluded for the season, especially if you race. Each time you go out you should check your mast again. Wire stretches and temperature and humidity may make a difference in a wooden mast. Wedges also tend to work loose. Racing skippers should try to find competition before the regular season begins to see whether their boats are really tuned properly.

Figure 124. **Cotter pins in the turnbuckles can tear sails and should always be wrapped in tape to protect their sharp points.**

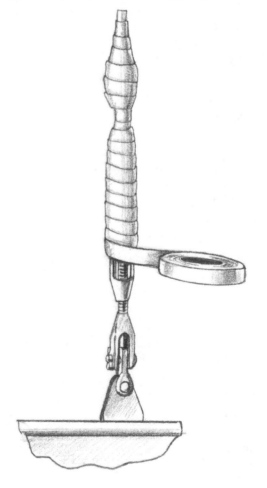

Figure 123. **When the boat is sharply heeled over, it is interesting to sight up the mast to see if it remains straight under pressure.**

Figure 125. Catamarans are very fast and provide many thrills at high speeds. Here the crew is suspended from a trapeze, getting weight as far out as possible for stability.

Handling the Multihull

There are two types of multihull sailboats, the *catamaran* and the *trimaran*. The catamaran is used almost exclusively as a day sailer, and features two slender hulls connected by some form of platform. The trimaran has a large center hull flanked by smaller outer hulls, and it is used for long-distance ocean cruising and racing. Both types of multihull boats are noted for their speed, which is often much more than the speed of a single-hull *(monohull)* of equivalent size. In addition to providing speed, the multihull arrangement has a great deal of stability in normal conditions, even though some small catamarans, like a Hobie Cat, often sail with the windward hull completely out of the water, when reaching or beating.

Handling a catamaran is not much different from handling a single-hull boat. While changing tacks, be certain the boat is already close-hauled and moving nicely through the water; it is of little use to try to come about if the boat is sailing off the wind or not moving well at the time.

The speed at which you turn into the wind is critical. If you turn too slowly, the boat will lose speed as sail drive is lost when heading nearly into the wind; there is a point where the sails are apparently drawing but in reality they are furnishing no drive at all. If you turn too rapidly, the rudders act as a brake and essential momentum is destroyed by drag.

As the boat continues to turn, hold the tiller at a 40-degree angle until the jib fills on the other tack.

As the boat begins coming into the eye of the wind, the mainsail can be hauled in perfectly flat in order to maintain drive as long as possible. However, keeping the main flat after the bow has passed through the eye of the wind can spoil the maneuver, as it will prevent the bow from falling off onto the new tack. Ease the main sheet as the boat passes through the wind.

There are some other factors: on a turbulent day, it is useless to turn directly into a breaking sea; wait for a comparatively smooth patch of water before coming about. It may be necessary to move your weight forward in order to keep the transoms from dragging, which can be a serious handicap at slow speeds. Be sure to handle the rudders gently; they can become brakes as well as steering devices. After some experience the helmsman can feel the point where turbulence begins to form about the rudder blade as he moves the tiller.

Sailors accustomed to single-hull sailing must learn to ease sail pressure when the weather hull of the catamaran starts to lift. Although it is exhilarating to sail with the windward hull airborne, sailing efficiency may be lost, and a sudden puff may push the boat past the point of stability, to a capsize.

Trimarans, a modern development of the double-outrigger craft of the Indonesians, are particularly suited to cruising, as ample headroom usually can be provided in the central hull, and storage spaces and accommodations may be found in the outrigger hulls. Several trimarans have circumnavigated the globe and have won major transoceanic races. Because of their wide beam and lack of a heavy keel (which can cause a pendulum action), there is very little roll action in a seaway. They usually sail at a small angle of heel, increasing comfort while cruising.

While the trimaran may be sailed at heeling angles that would cause other boats to capsize, remember that a trimaran is not self-righting like a single-hull boat with ballast. Some trimarans are fitted with a flotation device at the masthead so the boats cannot turn completely upside down, but even these are difficult to right.

Helpful Hint

THE GENOA AND VISIBILITY

Genoa jibs are often cut so that the foot of the sail comes right down to the deck of the boat. This is great for sailing speed, but it makes the helmsman's job of watching where he's going much more difficult. The helmsman must make a constant effort to glance around that genoa often, to see what other boats or obstructions might be there. In crowded waters it may be wise to station a crew member on the foredeck to watch ahead and "under" the genoa. Many a close call might be avoided by better vigilance around the genoa.

7

Marlinespike Seamanship

Line

Rope is purchased in a marine-supply store, where it is measured and sold from large spools or drums, or it may be sold in packages made up to convenient lengths. Once on board the boat, however, rope is known as *line*.

Coiling Line

When not in use on the boat, line is coiled neatly and compactly to prevent kinking, twisting, and knotting. These coils are readily made and quickly unmade should the line be needed in a hurry. Figure 126 shows the usual method of coiling line for stowage. The two drawings at the left show how the line is picked up and coiled in uniform loops; note that it is *handed* (coiled) in a clockwise

direction. The third and fourth drawings show how the line is bunched by wrapping the loose end around the coils. The fifth drawing shows how the loose end is then passed through the loop and pulled tight. When held by this end, the coil stays bunched and can be tossed into a locker.

Figure 127 shows another method of coiling line for stowage. The line is coiled and wrapped in the same manner as above, but a loop is made in the loose end which is passed through the upper part of the coil, as illustrated in the first drawing. Next the loop is passed over and around the coil and is allowed to fall to the level of the wraparound parts. The end is then pulled tight (third drawing) to keep the bundle set and secure. The loose end, passed through the top loop, serves as a carrying line. This type of coil is not likely to come loose or to ravel.

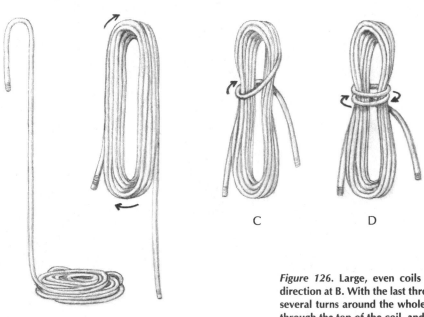

A   B   C   D   E

Figure 126. Large, even coils of line are made up in the same direction at B. With the last three feet of line, at C, make a collar of several turns around the whole coil, D. Then carry the tail of line through the top of the coil, and pull tight, E.

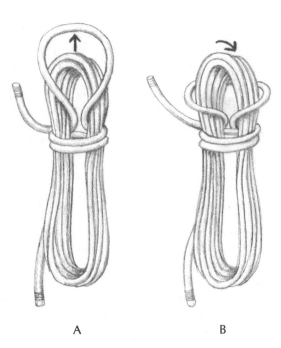

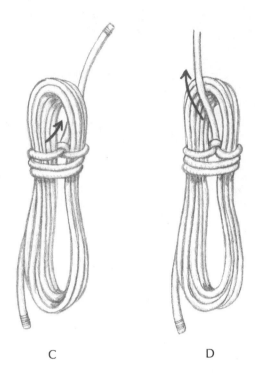

A   B   C   D

Figure 127. A second method of securing a coil of line is by making a loop in the final tail of the line, at A. The loop is thrown over the top of the coil, at B, then pulled tight at C. The tail now serves as a handle to hang the coil.

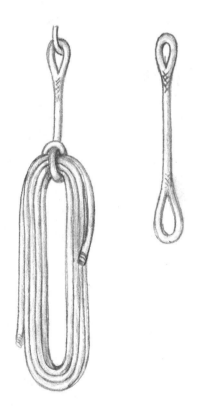

Figure 128. A handy loop can be made of spare line for hanging unused coils on a hook below deck.

Figure 128 shows a good method to use when line is to hang on the side of a bulkhead or locker. Here another line is brought into use; the short line with an eye splice at each end (drawing at right). This short line is passed through the loop of the coil, then one eye is passed through the other and pulled tight. The eye at the top is now free to serve as a loop for hanging the coil. This makes up into an exceptionally neat, tight bundle that keeps the loops from snarling and kinking.

Coiling the Halyard

After a sail has been hoisted, its halyard is coiled in the same clockwise manner as coiling a line for stowage. Gather the line in large even loops; when the line between the cleat and the coil gets short, a loop is made in this section (see Figure 129) and it is passed through the coil. This loop is then twisted a few times and hooked over the cleat as shown in the fourth drawing.

When the sail is to be lowered, the coils can quickly be removed from the cleat and laid on the deck, where they should run freely without snarling or twisting.

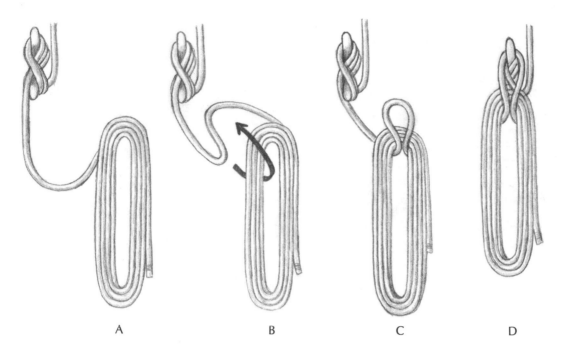

Figure 129. **To secure a halyard fall when a sail is raised, start coiling from the cleat, at A. Take the line that comes from the cleat, at B, pass it through the coil at C, and hook that part of line back on the cleat, at D.**

Heaving a Line

How a line is heaved is one of the marks that distinguishes the experienced sailor from the novice. The novice often coils the line wrong, and the end falls short of its mark. Properly coiled it can be cast easily and will run out without fouling. A few preparations, plus practice, will give you the seaman's touch.

First, the line must be much longer than the distance it is to be thrown; at least half again the distance. Otherwise, when thrown, it probably will fall short. Second, the line must be looped carefully and evenly, with the draw of the loops toward the hand holding the free end. The loops should be slightly smaller than those made for other purposes, in order to concentrate the weight of the line in the coil. A badly coiled line is hard to throw, generally fouls, has no carry-through, and will fall as a snarled lump.

Third, the coil must be held right for throwing. In most cases three quarters of the coil is held in the throwing hand, and the balance is held in the opposite hand, with the line leading directly from this hand to the coil without crossing or twisting

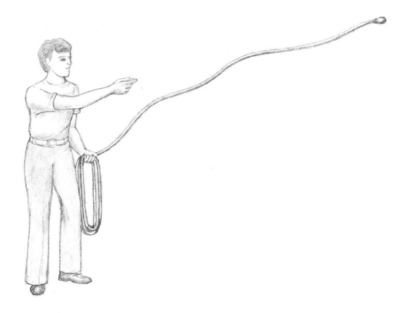

Figure 130. **Throwing a coil of line is more difficult than it looks. Remember to have enough line and to have neat, even coils to pay out as the line is thrown.**

over the loops. This allows the coils of the loop to open freely as the line runs out.

Fourth, the coil must be thrown properly, at the right moment, and at not too great a distance. Start by holding the coil low, at full arm's length. In an underhand motion, swing the throwing arm back; then throw with a stiff arm, achieving a strong swinging movement. When the coil is released, the arm should be well up above the shoulders. Aim at the head and shoulders and to one side of the person who is to receive the line. If the aim is at his feet or waist, the line is apt to fall short.

Figure 131. A light line with a weight on one end, called a monkey's fist, is often thrown first, then attached to a heavy line called a hawser, which is too heavy to throw. Once the light line is thrown and received, the hawser can follow.

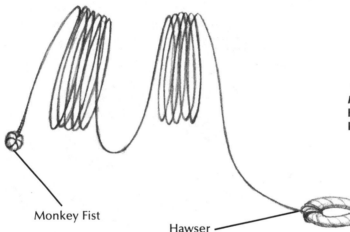

Monkey Fist

Hawser

Figure 132. Half of the coil to be thrown is kept in the throwing hand; the other half is allowed to run out with the toss. Note the long sweep with the throwing arm.

Knots and Splices

While there are more than a dozen knots and several types of splices that can be used aboard a sailboat, there are only three knots (and a variation of one of these) and one splice that should be in every sailor's marlinespike repertory. The knots are the *reef* or *square knot* and its variant, the *slippery reef knot,* the *bowline,* and the *anchor bend.* The splice is the *eye splice*.

Figure 134 illustrates the reef knot. Note that if line A were to pass over line B at the right of the second drawing, and line B then were to pass over, then under, line A in the third drawing, a *granny knot* would result. A reef knot will hold well when properly used and can be untied with little effort; the granny may come undone at the wrong time or jam when you want to untie it.

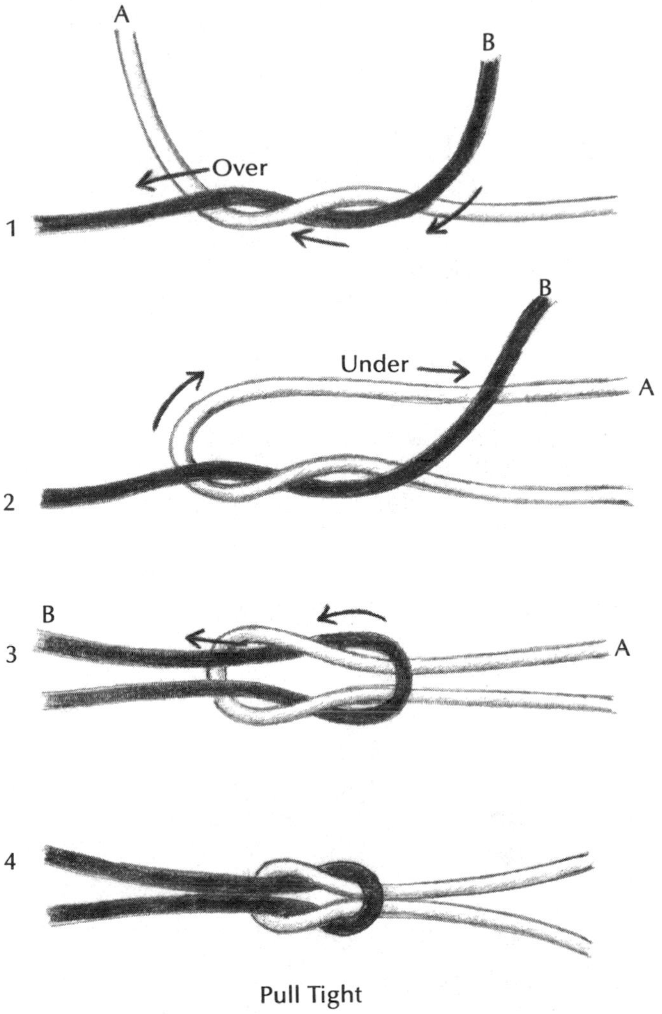

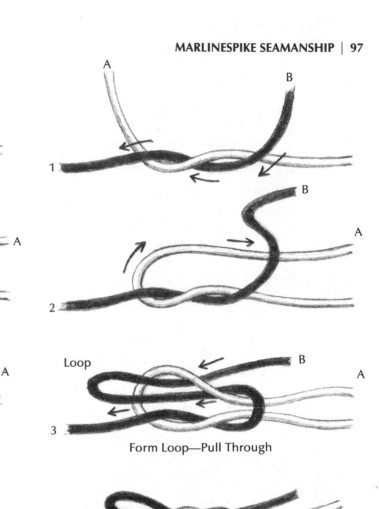

1 Over

2 Under →

3 B A

4 Pull Tight

Figure 133. A square knot is simple and strong. Be careful to avoid the weaker granny knot, described in the text.

1

2

3 Loop
Form Loop—Pull Through

4 Pull Tight—Be Sure Loop Does Not Draw Out

Figure 134. A reef knot or slippery knot can be released by a sharp tug on the end of the line B, a little like a shoelace knot.

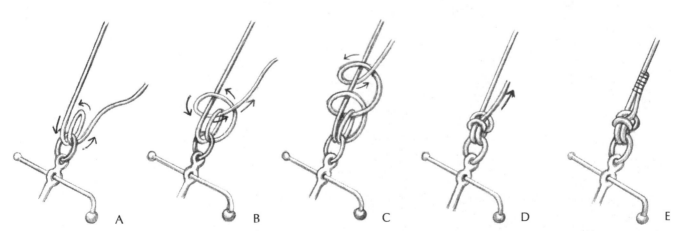

A   B   C   D   E

Figure 135. The anchor bend is strong and does not encourage chafe at the anchor ring. Note the extra security of a seizing, a few wraps of light line, at E.

Figure 136. A bowline is a sailor's best friend, strong, secure, and easy to untie even after being under extreme tension.

The slippery reef knot, Figure 134, is the same as a square knot, except that the loop left in the end of one line can be pulled to open the knot.

The anchor bend is shown in Figure 135 and is tied in the steps illustrated. This is a good substitute for an eye splice and shackle arrangement if the end of the line is seized to the standing part of the line.

A bowline, Figure 136, forms a loop that will not change size under any conditions. Small bowlines can be used to join ends of lines when a line of extra length is needed; a large bowline can be used for a loop to be slipped over a piling. The knot itself has great strength, yet it is easy to untie when there is no strain on the line.

An eye splice, like a bowline, can form a loop of any size. It is sometimes used at the end of permanent mooring lines, and in a small size, around a metal or plastic *thimble* at the end of a line where it is attached to an anchor. The eye splice is simple to make when working with three-strand line as shown in Figure 137, but be careful when making the first tuck with the third strand. The eye splice also can be made in double-braided line, using a special fid; the procedure is not as difficult as it might appear from the drawings.

For descriptions of other knots and splices and their uses, a text such as Charles F. Chapman's *Piloting, Seamanship & Small Boat Handling* is recommended.

Figure 137. A splice is a strong and permanent way to join two lines. In this eye splice, the size of the eye is determined at point X. Lines A, B, and C weave in and out as shown. The hardest part is at Step 3, at the first tucks. The final eye splice, at Step 4, should be even and smooth. Note how C, C[1], and C[2] weave evenly in successive tucks.

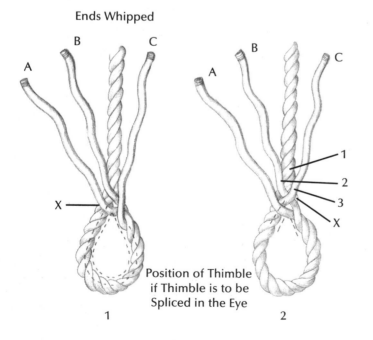

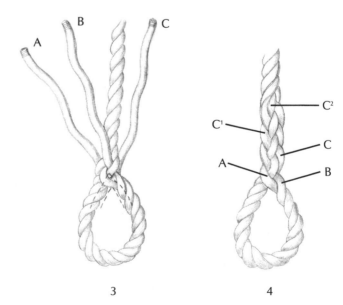

Helpful Hints

USING A CLEAT
Mooring lines, anchor lines, halyards, and any other lines must be cleated properly so that they will hold and yet be uncleated at any time, whether wet or dry, without trouble.

Here is the sequence to follow in cleating a line. Note that a full turn is taken around the base before the line crosses over a horn; note too that cleats should be fastened to the deck at a slight angle to the line of pull. This prevents the line from jamming. Usually a hitch is placed in the line on the last turn. It should cross neatly as shown. No more than one hitch should be necessary under any circumstances.

A

B

C

D

8

Legal Requirements

Whenever a boat of any size or type is in operation, there are certain government regulations that must be met regarding safety equipment to be carried, actions to be taken to avoid collision, and lights to be carried if the boat is to be operated at night. Note that many requirements that apply to powerboats do not apply to sailboats when they are under sail, but when a sailboat is under auxiliary power—using either an outboard or inboard engine—it is considered a powerboat, whether sails are raised or not.

Safety Equipment

For the purpose of establishing safety equipment requirements, boats are divided into size classes under provisions of the Motorboat Act of 1940. The classes and requirements are shown on page 104 for boats up to 26 feet in length, as well as additional classes for boats up to 65 feet in length; their requirements are detailed in reference texts such as Chapman's *Piloting, Seamanship & Small Boat Handling,* which is also published by Hearst Marine Books.

Common sense dictates that certain additional items, although not required by law, should be carried, depending on boat size and use. Such gear includes paddles or oars, a compass, charts, mooring line, anchor and anchor line, flashlight, bailer or pump, and emergency food and water.

Rules of the Road

Sailors should be very familiar with the two sets of rules of the road that govern actions to be taken to avoid collision and the lights to be carried by boats that operate at night. The United States Inland Rules cover all boats on the navigable waters of the United States except such small lakes and similar waterways that are entirely within the borders of a state and are not accessible from any interstate waterway. The International Rules of the Road cover boats operating outside of *demarcation lines* established at harbor entrances, between certain coastal headlands, and in other coastal areas where the distinction between inland and international waters must be made.

There is little significant difference between the two sets of rules for recreational craft, particularly for boats operating under sail alone. When two sailboats are converging on courses that might lead to a collision, one of them must keep clear in accordance with the following provisions:

1. When each has the wind on a different side, the one with the wind on her port side must keep out of the way of the other boat. The boat on the starboard tack has the right-of-way.
2. When both boats have the wind on the same side, the one that is to windward must keep out of the way of the boat that is to leeward. The leeward boat has the right-of-way.

3. If a boat is on the port tack and sees a boat to windward but cannot determine which tack this boat is on, she must keep clear of the boat to windward. Here the assumption is made that the boat to windward is on the starboard tack.

Sound signals are not exchanged when two sailboats are in these passing situations.

Because sailboats often operate with auxiliary power, the rules governing powerboat actions in passing situations should be known and understood. Less maneuverable vessels have right-of-way. This means that large ships, tugs with tows, and barges must be given right-of-way.

The overtaken vessel has right-of-way. If you are being passed by a faster vessel, hold a steady course, and the other vessel must go around you.

The Inland Rules of the Road provide for actions to be taken in three types of passing situations: meeting, crossing, and overtaking. When two powerboats are approaching head-on, or nearly so, it is a meeting situation. Neither boat has right-of-way; both must alter course to starboard and pass port side to port side. Either boat can signal first with one short whistle blast, which signifies "I plan to leave you on my port side." The other boat replies with the same signal.

A crossing situation exists when two boats are approaching each other not head-on, but each has the other forward of a direction 22½ degrees abaft the beam. In this case, the boat that has the other on her own starboard side must keep clear. It is the *give-way* vessel, in the language of the rules, or the burdened vessel. The boat that has the right-of-way is the *stand-on,* or privileged vessel.

The privileged vessel can signal with one short blast, indicating that she plans to leave the burdened vessel to port.

When one boat is approaching another from any point 22½ degrees or more abaft the overtaken boat's beam, it is an overtaking situation. The overtaking boat is the give-way vessel; the boat being overtaken is the stand-on vessel. She has the right-of-way and can maintain course and speed, although in some instances she may slow down or alter course to one side to allow more room for the overtaking boat to pass safely.

The overtaking boat signals her intent with one short blast if she intends to leave the overtaken boat on her port side, or two short blasts if she intends to leave the overtaken boat to starboard. The privileged vessel responds with the same signal if the overtaking vessel can pass safely on the proposed side. If this would be dangerous to either vessel, the privileged vessel responds with the *danger signal* of five or more short, rapid blasts. The overtaking boat remains behind until an exchange of signals indicates when and on which side it is safe to pass.

Note that under Inland Rules, whistle signals are signals of intent and are answered with the same signal to indicate that the intent is understood. Under International Rules, whistle signals are indications of steering action being taken and are sometimes called rudder signals. Under International Rules, one short blast indicates "I am altering course to starboard," and two short blasts indicates "I am altering course to port." Three short blasts in both sets of rules is used to indicate a boat is going into reverse. Under the International Rules, no reply is given to a whistle signal.

The meeting, crossing, and overtaking right-of-way provisions are the same under the International Rules, except for the exchange of signals. When overtaking, however, a boat first signals its intention by two long blasts, then the rudder signal to show which way it is altering course in order to pass the boat ahead.

Running Lights

Under both Inland and International Rules, boats less than 23 feet (7 meters) in length must carry an electric flashlight or a lantern that can be shown in time to prevent a collision. However, they may carry separate red and green sidelights (or a combination red and green bow light) and a white stern light—or the sidelights and stern light combined in a single masthead unit. Red light goes on the port side; green light on the starboard side on all boats. These lights must be carried on sailboats from 23 feet to 65.7 feet (20 meters) in length. If separate sidelights are carried, a sailboat can also carry a red light over a green light at or near the masthead.

A sailboat operating under power, with or without the sails raised, must show the running lights of a powerboat. This would be the separate or combination sidelights, the stern light, and a white masthead light.

For additional information on running lights for vessels of all types, Chapman's *Piloting, Seamanship & Small Boat Handling* is recommended.

Helpful Hints

BASIC GUIDES TO BOATING SAFETY

1. Carry proper equipment—know how to use it.
2. Maintain boat and equipment in top condition.
3. Know and obey the Rules of the Road.
4. Operate with care, courtesy, and common sense.
5. Always keep your boat under complete control.
6. Watch posted speeds; slow down in anchorages.
7. Do not *ever* overload your boat.
8. See that lifesaving equipment is accessible.
9. Check local weather reports before departure.
10. Inspect hull, engine, and all gear frequently.
11. Keep bilges clean, electrical contacts tight.
12. Guard rigidly against any fuel system leakage.
13. Have fire extinguishers instantly available.
14. Take maximum precautions when taking on fuel.
15. Be sure to allow adequate scope when anchoring.
16. Request a USCG Auxiliary Courtesy Marine Examination.
17. Enroll in a U.S. Power Squadrons or Coast Guard Auxiliary boating class.

REQUIRED ON-BOARD EQUIPMENT

All boats must carry readily accessible personal flotation devices (PFDs) for each person on board. In addition, all boats must be able to make sound signals, although the requirements for bells, whistles, and horns vary with the size of the vessel. Visual signaling devices, which vary in type relative to daytime and nighttime usage, are also required.

Any boat with an inboard engine or any boat with enclosed cabin space and an outboard motor must have one or more fire extinguishers, the number and type of which depend on the size and the usage of the boat.

Navigation lights are also imperative; the type necessary varies with the size and type of boat. A very small sailboat must carry at least a flashlight.

Full information on the required types of lights, fire extinguishers, and PFDs for each size and type of pleasure boat is given in Chapman's *Piloting, Seamanship & Small Boat Handling*. Many other important items of equipment—anchors, compasses, dock lines, charts, and flashlights—are not specified by law because their usage varies.

Minimum Required Equipment

EQUIPMENT	CLASS A (Less than 16 feet)	CLASS 1 (16 feet to less than 26 feet)	CLASS 2 (26 feet to less than 40 feet)	CLASS 3 (40 feet to not more than 65 feet)
BACKFIRE FLAME ARRESTER	One approved device on each carburetor of all gasoline engines installed after April 25, 1940, except outboard motors.			
VENTILATION	At least two ventilator ducts fitted with cowls or their equivalent for the purpose of properly and efficiently ventilating the bilges of every engine and fuel-tank compartment of boats constructed or decked over after April 25, 1940, using gasoline or other fuel of a flash point less than 110° F.			
BELL	None.*	None.*	One, which when struck, produces a clear, bell-like tone of full round characteristics.	
PERSONAL FLOTATION DEVICES	One Type I, II, III, or IV for each person.	One Type I, II, or III for each person on board or being towed on water skis, etc., plus one Type IV available to be thrown.		
WHISTLE	None.*	One hand, mouth, or power operated, audible at least ½ mile.	One hand or power operated, audible at least 1 mile.	One power operated, audible at least 1 mile.
FIRE EXTINGUISHER— PORTABLE				
When NO fixed fire extinguishing system is installed in machinery space(s).	At least One B-1 type approved hand portable fire extinguisher. (Not required on outboard motorboat less than 26 feet in length and not carrying passengers for hire if the construction of such motorboats will not permit the entrapment of explosive or flammable gases or vapors.)		At least Two B-1 type approved hand portable fire extinguishers; OR at least One B-11 type approved hand portable fire extinguisher.	At least Three B-1 type approved hand portable fire extinguishers; OR at least One B-1 type plus One B-11 type approved hand portable fire extinguisher.
When fixed fire extinguishing system is installed in machinery space(s).	None.	None.	At least One B-1 type approved hand portable fire extinguisher.	At least Two B-1 type approved hand portable fire extinguishers; OR at least One B-11 type approved hand portable fire extinguisher.
	Note: Dry Chemical and Carbon Dioxide (CO_2) are the most widely used types, in that order. The others, while acceptable, are seldom seen on boats.			
	Fire extinguishers manufactured after 1 January 1965 will be marked, "Marine Type USCG Type———Size———Approval No. 162.028/EX . . ."**			

*NOTE.—Not required by the Motorboat Act of 1940; however, the "Rules of the Road" require these vessels to sound proper signals.

**NOTE.—Toxic vaporizing-liquid type fire extinguishers, such as those containing carbon tetrachloride or chlorobromomethane, are not accepted as required approved extinguishers on uninspected vessels (private pleasure craft).

Beaufort Scale of Wind and Water

BEAUFORT NO.		M.P.H.	KNOTS	WIND DESCRIPTION	EFFECT OF WIND ON SEA	EFFECT OF WIND ON BOATS 15 TO 40 FT.
Force	0	Less than 1		Calm	Sea smooth and glassy	Becalmed; no steerageway; sails slat
Force	1	1-3	1-3	Light air	Ripples; surface is ruffled by wind; some smooth patches may remain	Sufficient way on for steering; sails take airfoil shape loosely
Force	2	4-7	4-6	Light breeze	Entire surface ruffled; small wavelets short but pronounced; crests glassy	Boats sail easily and begin to heel
Force	3	8-12	7-10	Gentle breeze	Large wavelets; occasional whitecaps	Good sailing
Force	4	13-18	11-16	Moderate breeze	Small waves, becoming longer; about half the waves show whitecaps	Small boats shorten sail; large ones carry working sails, genoas
Force	5	19-24	17-21	Fresh breeze	Moderate waves of a pronounced long form; most crests show whitecaps; some spray	Small boats, reefed mainsail only; large boats shorten sail
Force	6	25-31	22-27	Strong breeze	Large waves begin to form; whitecaps everywhere; foam and spray	Small boats return to port; larger craft double reef
Force	7	32-38	28-33	Moderate gale	Sea heaps up; white foam from crests blows in streaks	Storm canvas
Force	8	39-46	34-40	Fresh gale	Moderately high waves; edges of crests spume; heavier streaks of foam	Bare poles; lie ahull or run off with great care
Force	9	47-54	41-47	Strong gale	High waves; dense streaks of foam; spray may affect visibility	Lie to sea anchor or run off, streaming drogue
Force	10	55-63	48-55	Whole gale	Very high waves with long overhanging crests; great foam patches; much spray	Lie to sea anchor
Force	11	64-72	56-63	Storm	Exceptionally high waves; foam patches cover sea; wave crests blown into froth	Seek shelter if possible
Force	12	73+	64+	Hurricane (Atlantic) Typhoon (Pacific)	Air filled with foam and spray; sea completely white with driving spray	Seek shelter if possible

The Beaufort Scale is used to describe the wind strengths and wave conditions at sea. It is useful in understanding what conditions to expect when you hear a weather prediction.

Glossary

Abaft: When on board, astern of; *i.e.,* the mizzenmast is abaft the mainmast.

Abeam: At right angles to the centerline of the boat, but not on the boat.

Accidental jibe: When the mainsail swings unexpectedly to the opposite side while a boat is sailing downwind; a potentially dangerous maneuver.

Aft: Near, or toward, the stern of the boat.

Alee: Away from the direction of the wind, usually referring to the movement of the helm or tiller.

Amidships: The center part of a vessel between bow and stern; also, that part of the vessel between the port and starboard sides.

Apparent wind: The wind that makes a boat sail; its strength and direction are those of the true wind as modified by the wind created by the boat's forward movement over the water (see *True wind*).

Astern: Opposite of *ahead;* behind a boat.

Athwartships: Across a boat from side to side.

Backing: The wind is said to be backing when it changes direction counterclockwise.

Backstay: Rigging that supports the mast from aft.

Backwind: Wind deflected by a boat's sail into the leeward side of another sail is said to backwind the sail.

Bail: A metal half-hoop used to hold a block to a boom.

Ballast: Additional weight, sometimes as much as half of the boat's entire weight, placed in the lowest part of the boat, usually the keel.

Battens: Wood or plastic stiffeners placed in pockets in the leech of a sail to keep the edge from curling over.

Beam: The greatest width of a vessel.

Beam reach: Sailing with the apparent wind coming at right angles to the boat.

Bear down: Approach from windward.

Bearing: The direction of an object relative to a boat or as a true bearing as shown on a chart.

Bear off: Change course and sail to leeward.

Beating: Sailing to windward in a series of tacks; sometimes used to mean simply sailing close-hauled or upwind.

Beaufort Scale: A system of describing wind and sea conditions by number, from 0 for flat calm to 12 for a hurricane.

Before the wind: In the same direction as the wind is blowing.

Belay: Make fast a line to a cleat or belaying pin; also a verbal command to rescind a previous order or to stop an action being carried out.

Below: Beneath the deck.

Bend: A knot that fastens one line to another; also, as a verb, to attach a sail to a spar or stay.

Bight: Any part of a rope between the ends, but usually a loop.

Binnacle: A stand or case holding a boat's compass.

Blanketed: When a sail is between the wind and another sail, the latter cannot get wind and is said to be blanketed. One boat can blanket another boat by sailing between it and the wind.

Block: The nautical word for pulley.

Board boat: A small sailboat with only one sail; the crew usually sits on the boat rather than inside it.

Board Sailer: A one-person, surfboardlike boat with a wishbone sail. Often called a Windsurfer, a trade name.

Bolt rope: A line attached to and forming part of the foot or the luff of a sail to give it strength or to substitute for sail slides.

Boom: A spar to which the foot of a sail is attached. The boom itself is attached to a mast or to a stay.

Boom Crotch: A board with a notch cut in one end, into which the boom drops snugly.

Boom vang: A tackle running between boom and deck (or base of the mast) that flattens the sail's curve by a downward pull on the boom.

Boot top: The waterline stripe.

Bow: The forward part of a boat.

Bow Chock: Metal fittings at the bow, having openings through which a line (generally an anchor or dock line) is passed.

Bowsprit: A spar extending forward of the bow and set into the deck to support the headsails.

Breakwater: An artificial embankment to protect anchorages or harbor entrances.

Broach: Swing out of control so that a boat is broadside to the wind and waves. Broaching can cause dangerous heeling and damage to rigging.

Broad reach: Sailing with the wind coming over either quarter of the boat.

Burdened vessel: A vessel that, in accordance with right-of-way rules, is required to change course or speed to avoid collision with another vessel.

By the lee: With the wind on the same side as the main boom while a boat is running; considered potentially dangerous because it invites an accidental jibe.

Cam cleat: A small spring-loaded device for holding lines under load.

Cast off: To unfasten a line; to unfasten all dock lines when leaving a dock.

Catamaran: A boat with twin parallel hulls.

Catboat: A sailboat with a single mast, stepped far forward, carrying one sail only (no headsails).

Centerboard: A plate or board that can be raised or lowered through a slot in the bottom of the boat. It provides lateral resistance against the water to prevent the boat from making leeway or sideslipping.

Chafe: Wear on a sail, spar, or line caused by rubbing against something while in use. It can be prevented by chafing gear, which absorbs the friction.

Chain plate: A metal strap bolted to the side of a sailboat, to which a shroud or stay is attached.

Chock: A U-shaped fitting, usually metal, secured in or on a boat's rail, through which anchoring and mooring lines are led. An open fairlead.

Cleat: A double-horned fitting of wood or metal to which lines are secured, or *made fast*.

Clew: The lower, after corner of a sail.

Close-hauled: A boat is said to be close-hauled when she is sailing as close as possible to the wind.

Close reach: Said of a boat when she is sailing with sheets eased but with the wind forward of the beam.

Cockpit: The area of a boat from which she is steered.

Coming About: Bringing the boat from one tack to the other when sailing on the wind.

Cotter pin: A metal pin, doubled so the ends can be spread after it is inserted in a hole or slot; it is used to hold a metal fitting in place. A circular split ring is often used in place of a cotter pin.

Cringle: A ring sewn into a sail, through which a line may be passed.

Cunningham: A special cringle that is used with a line to alter and control the draft, or shape, of a mainsail.

Current: The horizontal movement of water, caused by the tide or wind or both. (See *Tide*.)

Daggerboard: A type of removable centerboard that does not pivot but is raised and lowered vertically.

Displacement: The weight of water displaced by a floating vessel; hence, the weight of the vessel itself.

Downhaul: Tackle attached to the underside of a sliding gooseneck; it tightens the sail's luff by pulling down on the boom.

Draft: The depth of water at the lowest point of a vessel's keel.

Ease: Slacken; applies to sheets and other lines as well as to wind, weather, and current.

Eye of the wind: The direction from which the wind is coming.

Eye splice: A permanent loop in the end of a rope made by splicing, or weaving, the end of the rope back on itself.

Fairlead: A fitting that controls or changes the direction of a line.

Fall off: To allow a boat's bow to turn away from the wind.

Fathom: Six feet, usually seen as a measurement of depth on charts.

Fender: A cushion placed between boats or between a boat and a dock to prevent marring the hull.

Foot: The lower edge of a sail.

Fore and Aft: In the direction of the keel.

Forestay: A stay running from the mast down to the foredeck inside the jibstay on a vessel, such as a cutter, that carries more than one headsail. The forestaysail is hoisted on it.

Forward: Toward the bow.

Fouled: Tangled or caught; said of a line or an anchor.

Freeboard: The vertical distance from the waterline to the gunwale at its lowest point.

Gaff: A spar supporting the head of a four-sided fore-and-aft sail.

Gasket: A strip of dacron or other material used for tying up the sails; also called a *stop*.

Genoa: A large jib that overlaps the mast.

Ghosting: A sailboat moving in little or no wind is said to be ghosting.

Gooseneck: The fitting that secures a boom to the mast; it can be fixed or can slide up and down.

Ground tackle: A collective term for the anchor and associated gear—cable, chain, swivel, etc.

Gudgeon and pintle: A socket and pin, by which a rudder is fastened to a boat.

Gunwale: The rail of a boat, i.e., the upper edge of a boat's hull; pronounced "gun'l."

Halyard: A line or wire used for hoisting sails.

Hank: A fitting for attaching a sail to a stay; a clip or snap hook.

"Hard-a-lee": A command given to begin tacking, or coming about, accompanied by the action of pushing the tiller to leeward.

Head: The upper corner of a triangular sail. Also, the toilet facilities on a boat.

Head down; head off: To head away from the wind; the opposite of *head up*.

Headsails: Sails set forward of the foremost mast; includes jibs and staysails.

Head up: Steer a boat closer to the direction from which the wind is coming; the opposite of *head down* or *head off*.

Heave to: A useful and safe method of riding through moderately heavy weather by backing the sails and securing the tiller or wheel.

Heel: A vessel that leans to one side, by wind pressure in the normal course of sailing, is said to heel.

Helm: The tiller or steering wheel; the steering apparatus and its effect.

Hitch: A method of making a rope fast to another rope or to a spar.

In irons: A sailboat is said to be in irons when she is head to wind with no steerageway.

Jam cleat: A device with a V-shaped opening to hold a sheet or other line.

Jib: A triangular sail set forward of the foremost mast.

Jibe: Bring the wind to the opposite side of the boat when sailing downwind, so that the sails swing to the other side; the proper command is "Jibe ho!" (See also *Accidental jibe.*)

Jibsheet: The line that runs from the clew of the jib to the cockpit or deck, used to control the sail.

Jibstay: The forward stay on which the jib is hoisted.

Jiffy Reefing: Method of reducing sail similar to traditional reefing, without the dependence on individual reef points.

Keel: The deepest part of a vessel, the structural section that protrudes beneath the main part of the hull. A keel boat has a permanent keel to prevent leeway, as opposed to a centerboard.

Ketch: A two-masted sailboat on which the mizzenmast (the aftermost mast) is shorter than the mainmast and is stepped forward of the rudder post.

Knockdown: The action and result when a boat is laid over suddenly by wind or sea, so that water pours over the gunwale.

Knot: A measure of speed equal to one nautical mile (6,076 feet) per hour.

Lay a mark: To be able to reach a mark, when sailing close-hauled, without tacking. *Lay* also refers to the direction in which the strands of a rope are twisted.

Lead block: A pulley used to control a guy or sheet; the lead block is often a snatch block (see *Snatch block*).

Leech: The after, or rear, edge of a sail.

Lee helm: The tendency of a boat under sail to turn away from the wind when the helm is amidships. (See also *Weather helm.*)

Leeward: The direction away from that in which the wind is blowing; pronounced "lu'ard."

Leeway: The drift a boat makes to leeward when she is sailing at an angle to the wind.

Lift: A rigging line used to control or hold a boom or spinnaker pole.

List: The leaning of a vessel to one side due to uneven distribution of weight.

Loose-footed: Said of a sail that is secured to the boom at the tack and clew only.

Lubber line: A mark inside the compass, representing a boat's heading.

Luff: As a noun, the forward edge of a sail; as a verb, to head a boat up into the wind, thus causing the sail to flutter; the fluttering of the sail is called luffing.

Mainmast: The tallest mast on a boat.

Mainsail: The sail set abaft the mainmast; pronounced "mains'l."

Mainsheet: The line controlling the mainsail.

Marlinespike: A tool for opening the strands of a rope or wire while splicing it.

Mast: The vertical pole or spar supporting the booms, gaffs, and sails.

Masthead: The top of the mast.

Mast step: The strong brace or fitting on which the bottom of a mast rests.

Mizzen: The after and smaller mast of a ketch or yawl; also, the sail set on that mast.

Mooring: A place to tie a boat up to, usually a semipermanent anchor and gear (chain, float, pendant, swivel) left in place in the water.

Off the wind: Sailing with the wind abeam or astern.

Outhaul: A device on the boom for stretching the foot of the sail out along the boom from the mast.

Overhaul: Remove kinks and snarls from a line.

Painter: Dinghy towrope or dockline.

Pendant: A control line for a pivoting centerboard or a movable rudder blade; the rope portion of a permanent mooring attached to the pick-up buoy or float. Pronounced "pennant."

Pennant: A small flag, often used to indicate wind direction.

Pinching: Sailing a boat closer to the wind than she can efficiently go.

Pintle: See *Gudgeon.*

Pointing: Sailing close to the wind.

Point of sailing: The direction of the boat in relation to the wind: beating, reaching, or running (see individual terms).

Port: The left side of a vessel, looking forward, or the direction to the left.

Port tack: Sailing with the wind coming over a boat's port side.

Privileged vessel: One that has the right of way.

Pulpit: An elevated tubular metal guardrail at the bow or stern.

Quarter: Either side of a boat, from the stern to amidships.

Rake: The angle of a vessel's mast from the perpendicular; a mast usually rakes aft.

Reach: The point of sailing between close-hauled and running, with the wind abeam.

"Ready about": The order given to alert the crew before tacking. (The next order is "Hard-a-lee.")

Reef: Reduce the area of the sail.

Reef points: Short lines set in rows along the sail, used for reefing.

Rigging screw: See *Turnbuckle*.

Roach: The extra area in the curved leech of a sail; beyond a straight line from head to clew.

Rode: Anchor line.

Roller furling: A method of rolling a jib up on its stay.

Roller reefing: A method of reefing the mainsail in which the sail is wound up by rotating the boom.

Rudder: A movable, flat device hinged vertically at the stern of a boat as a means of steering. It is controlled by the tiller or wheel.

Running: Sailing with the wind astern.

Running rigging: Sheets, halyards, guys, lifts and other frequently adjusted lines.

Schooner: A vessel with two or more masts carrying fore-and-aft sails. If two-masted, the foremast is shorter than the mainmast.

Scope: The ratio of length of anchor line used to depth of water; expressed as "5 to 1," etc.

Sculling: Moving the tiller back and forth quickly to move the boat ahead.

Secure: Make fast.

Seize: Bind with a thin line.

Shackle: A metal link, usually U-shaped, with a pin that unscrews to open the shackle so that it can be attached to a line, a sail, or a fitting; a snap shackle has a spring-loaded pin that unlocks to open the shackle.

Shaking out: Untying a reef.

Sheave: The wheel inside a block or at the masthead or mast foot, on which a line turns; pronounced: "shiv."

Sheet: A line used to trim a sail.

Shock cord: Strong elastic line used for special rigging purposes such as keeping a topping lift out of the way of a sail.

Shroud: Standing rigging that supports a mast at the sides.

Sloop: A single-masted sailboat whose principal sails are a main and a jib.

Snatch block: A block that opens at the side so that a line can be hooked into it without threading the entire line.

Sounding line: A line marked to measure the depth of water. Attached to the end is a weight or lead. Often called a lead line.

Spars: A general term for masts, booms, poles, gaffs, etc. that hold sails extended.

Spinnaker: A light headsail used in running and reaching and shaped a bit like a parachute.

Splice: Join two ropes permanently by weaving their strands together alternately over and under each other.

Spreaders: Bars fastened aloft on a mast to increase the angle of the shrouds.

Spring line: A long dock line that prevents movement, forward or aft, of a docked boat.

Squall: A sudden and violent gust of wind often accompanied by rain or snow.

Standing part: The fixed part of a rope or line that takes the strain, as opposed to the free ends or the bight.

Standing rigging: The shrouds and stays supporting the mast.

Starboard: The right side of the vessel, facing forward, or the direction to the right.

Stay: Rigging supporting the mast from forward or aft.

Staysail: Any of various fore-and-aft sails, usually triangular but sometimes quadrilateral, generally set in addition to or inside the boat's other sails, e.g., forestaysail, spinnaker staysail, mizzen staysail, fisherman staysail; pronounced: "stays'l."

Steerageway: A boat has steerageway when she is moving through the water with enough speed so that the rudder can control and change her direction.

Stern: The back of a boat.

Stops: Tape, sewn cloth strips, or short pieces of line used to hold a sail in place after it is furled.

Storm jib: A small triangular sail at the bow of the boat, used in very heavy weather.

Sweated up: A laborious but effective method of raising a sail that last few inches without using winches. Crew member pulls out from mast while halyard is secured under a cleat; slack is taken up quickly at the cleat.

Tack: As a noun, the lower forward corner of a sail. The way in which a boat is moving with respect to the wind, i.e., a boat is on a port or starboard tack depending on which side the wind is from. As a verb, to come about, or turn the bow of the boat through the eye of the wind.

Tacking: Changing tacks, or coming about; sailing upwind on a zig-zag course so that the boat is alternately on a port and a starboard tack.

Tackle: Ropes and blocks rigged together for hauling; pronounced "tayk'l."

Tang: A fitting, usually on the upper part of a mast, to which a stay or shroud is made fast.

Telltale: A wind-direction indicator made of cloth, yarn, or feather, fastened to a shroud or sail.

Thwart: A seat extending across a boat.

Tide: The vertical movement of water caused by the gravitational pull of the sun and moon. (See also *Current*.)

Tiller: The long lever by which the rudder is moved.

Topping lift: An adjustable line from the masthead to the end of the boom; used to hold up the boom when the sail is not set. Also called a *boom lift*.

True wind: The actual direction and speed of the wind, as opposed to the apparent direction and speed. (See also *Apparent wind*.)

Turnbuckle or *rigging screw*: A mechanical device for adjusting the tension on stays and shrouds.

Under way: Said of a boat moving and under control of the helmsman. (Technically, a vessel is under way when not aground, at anchor, or made fast to the shore.)

Vang: See *Boom vang*.

Veering: Wind veers when its direction changes in a clockwise direction.

Warp: Move or turn a boat around a dock or pilings, using dock lines and spring lines.

Way on: The movement of a boat through the water.

Weather helm: The tendency of a boat, with her rudder amidships, to turn by herself to windward. (See also *Lee helm*.)

Weather side: The upwind side.

Whipping: A binding of light line or tape on the end of a line to keep it from fraying.

Winch: A drum-shaped device around which a line is coiled; it provides mechanical advantage when a line is being brought in under load.

Windward: The general direction from which the wind is coming.

Wing and wing: A boat is said to be sailing wing and wing when she is sailing downwind with the mainsail and jib set and filled on opposite sides of the boat.

Yawl: A two-masted vessel whose mizzen is small and stepped abaft the rudder post.

Index